PLUM CREE

Prairie Sampler

Johanna Wilson

©2003 Johanna Wilson

Published by

kp **krause publications**
An F&W Publications Company

700 East State Street • Iola, WI 54990-0001
715-445-2214 • 888-457-2873
www.krause.com

Please call or write for our free catalog of publications. Our toll-free
number to place an order or obtain a free catalog is 800-258-0929, or
please use our regular business telephone 715-445-2214.

Illustrations by Ormon Wilson.

Manufactured in China

Library of Congress Catalog Number: 2002113161

ISBN: 0-87349-542-X

dedication

To Ormon, the gentle man who has shared my life and endured my passion for quilts with much understanding and great patience…and draws wonderful illustrations for my projects.

acknowledgments

A big **Thank You** to all the quilters who made the quilts and to those who quilted the quilts for this book. Thanks also, to each quilter who will make these quilts in the future and to Henrietta, who made the first quilt.

Thanks to all who offered technical assistance: Sandy Alexander, Ruth Hewitt, Galen McCarthy, Carol Steiner, and Shirley Wilson. Special thanks to Karla Schulz.

table of contents

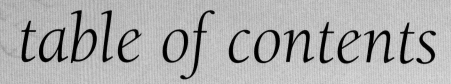

Welcome from the banks of Plum Creek! We're celebrating our tenth year with— *Plum Creek Prairie Sampler.*

Who would have thought when we moved to our prairie farm in Walnut Grove, Minnesota, many years ago that we would eventually become farmer/quilters? It was the second or third long winter with short cold days and long cold nights. It was then that I rediscovered an ancient quilt top given to me in Connecticut by a dear friend. Three generations of hands had cherished this quilt top. I had carried it halfway across the country before attempting to complete the project. This inherited gift of Henrietta's quilt changed my life on the prairie. Quilting lore unfolded and fabric patterns emerged.

The entire process engaged my curiosity. How were blocks made? What were they called? What designs were possible? This curiosity remains today as I search for unusual blocks to use in quilts such as this Prairie Sampler, a quilt with many blocks of different sizes set together like a puzzle. These eleven blocks inspired me to explore and create a myriad of designs—enough to fill a book! Many of the quilts in this Prairie Sampler are those made by women attending my annual quilt retreats in Minnesota.

With this book, you can share the community we found by creating your personal quilt retreat at home. You can make a quilt similar to the Prairie Sampler or any one of the many other projects included in this book, assisted by step-by-step directions and dozens of color illustrations.

Happy stitching from
Plum Creek Patchwork!

Quilt Beginnings ...

▶Fabric Selection

Plum Creek
Patchwork
Retreat 2001

For some of you, choosing the fabric for your quilt is the most exciting and rewarding part of a quilting project. For others, choosing fabric can be an exhausting and terrifying experience. Here are a few suggestions to help build your confidence and make the task more enjoyable.

- Purchase the best quality fabric you can afford. This is the first step toward making a great quilt that will be worth the time you spend creating it.
- Begin by choosing a fabric you love and add other fabrics to enhance the first.
- Try to visualize the fabrics relative to the size they will be in the quilt.

- Vary the size of the fabric designs (scale) you have chosen to keep your eye moving around the quilt.
- Consider including a "new color," a plaid, stripe, or large print to add interest to your work.
- Any fabrics you buy that are not perfect for the current quilt project enhance your fabric collection.
- It is your quilt project so choose fabrics you like.
- You have better color sense than you think. Remember you choose your wardrobe, your home décor, and flowers for your garden.

▶Design Area

Create a design area to help you make color choices. You can use a wall, the back of a door or a large piece of cardboard covered with flannel or cotton batting. Place it in a location where you can stand back several feet to audition your fabric. You will be amazed at how helpful this will be in making choices.

▶Accuracy

Cutting and sewing accurately can make the quilting process a much more pleasurable experience. Adequate lighting is necessary for accuracy in cutting and stitching. Treat yourself to a good light source for your cutting table, your machine sewing area, and your favorite spot for handwork.

Cutting fabric

Careful and accurate cutting is essential to quilt construction. You will need a self healing cutting mat to cut on, a rotary cutter for cutting and acrylic rulers for measuring fabric and to use as a cutting guide. Be sure you can read the numbers on the ruler before purchasing. There are many rotary cutters and dozens of rulers in many shapes and sizes available.

- A cutting table set at the proper height is important for maintaining a healthy back.
- Experiment to find the rotary cutter and ruler most comfortable for you. To ensure accuracy, use the same ruler throughout your project.
- A rotary cutter often looks like a pizza cutter and can be dangerous if not handled very carefully.
- As you cut strips, always cut away from your body. Hold down on the ruler with one hand, cutting along the edge with the rotary cutter only as far as the tips of your fingers. Then move your hand ahead and continue cutting. Check for a satisfactory cut before moving the ruler.
- Be sure to close the blade every time you put the cutter down.
- Does your blade need replacing? Add new rotary blades to your supply list.

- The 6" and 12" rulers are good choices to use when cutting small pieces with the rotary cutter. The 24" ruler is a good choice for cutting strips of fabric across the folded width of fabric (WOF).

Above. Retreaters look on as Master Quilter, Karla Schulz, concentrates on quilting her quilt.

Left. This quilter uses adequate lighting to help her make expert stitches.

Below: Measure twice. Cut once!

Quarter-Inch Seams

Quilt patterns require a scant ¼" seam allowance. Check your accuracy by cutting three pieces 1½" x 4" and sewing them together along the 4" side. Press the seams to one side, and then lay a ruler over the strips on the right side to check the size. Your piece should measure 3½" across with the center strip exactly 1". If it doesn't, cut new strips, adjust the seams, and repeat until you have found your correct measurement. Even if your machine has a ¼" foot, check the seam allowance the same way. You may be able to adjust the needle position to make adjustments. Mark your perfect seam allowance on the machine bed with a marking pen or a piece of tape. Always use this guide when sewing quilt seams. Blue painters masking tape and black electrical tape will not leave a residue on your machine.

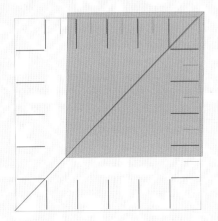

Pressing

Press pieces flat after each seam is sewn as they come from the sewing machine. Open the pieces, holding the darker side in one hand so that the lighter side including the seam is flat on the pressing board. Place the iron on the right side along the seam line, and hold it in place for a few seconds. This will automatically press the seam toward the darker fabric. Pick up the iron and put it down until you have reached the end of the seam. Remember to press, not iron, the pieces. Ironing is moving the iron in a back and forth motion, which can easily distort small pieces of fabric. Pressing from the right side helps avoid pressing pleats into the seam and distorting the size. Trim as necessary.

Trimming

Check the size of your pieced blocks as you press. The sizes for the pieces are given in parentheses, for example (2½" x 4½"), as you proceed through the patterns. Check the size after you press, and square up the block if necessary. Trimming to size will help keep the pieces square as you sew to the next piece, eliminating excess frustration! Check the seam allowance frequently.

Un-sewing or ripping out

Occasionally, a seam may be too large, or we may sew the pieces together incorrectly, which leads to reverse manual sewing better know as ripping or un-sewing.

To un-sew, use a sharp seam ripper and carefully cut every third or fourth stitch along one side of the seam to be removed. Turn to the other side of the seam, and gently lift the uncut thread with the dull side of the ripper. You should be able to loosen the entire seam.

If your stitches are very close together, you might want to adjust your stitch length on the sewing machine. Very small stitches are more difficult to rip out!

Press, don't iron!

Sometimes it's necessary to un-sew.

▶Basic Quilting Techniques

Basic quilting techniques used throughout the book are explained in this section. They may be used as a reference for unfamiliar techniques or to brush up on familiar techniques as you read through the pattern directions.

In the piecing directions, quilts with multiple sizes have the number of pieces or the sizes needed for each step. For example, a notation of "4, (20, 48)" indicates that a wall quilt will need four pieces for each step, a twin quilt will need 20, and a queen size quilt will need 48.

Strip Piecing

The invention of the rotary cutter introduced a quick and easy method of cutting strips the width of the fabric (WOF). Strip piecing is used for piecing some Four Patch, Windmill, and Checkerboard blocks and borders.

1 Cut strips the size indicated in the pattern.

2 Place strips rights sides together, and sew seam along the long side. Press toward the darker fabric.

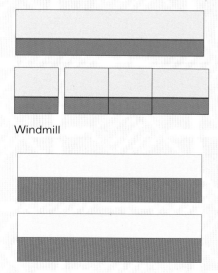

Windmill

Checkerboard

3 Cut pieces from the strips, the size indicated, to be used in blocks or borders.

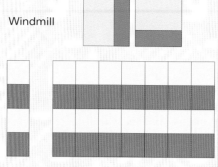

Windmill

Checkerboard

4 Rearrange the cut segments, and then sew them together to make the blocks.

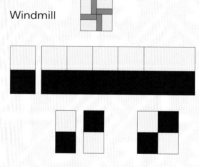

Windmill

Four Patch

Half-Square Triangles

To increase accuracy in making half-square triangles, I like to make the half square triangle then "trim to size" indicated in the pattern.

1 Place the strips of fabric with right sides together.

2 Cut squares from both strips at the same time, making them the size indicated in the pattern.

3 Cut the pairs of squares in half diagonally. Chain stitch the pairs of triangles along the bias edge, feeding them in the sewing machine one pair

after the other without cutting the thread.

4 Press flat as they come from the machine, and then cut the triangles apart.

5 Open right side up and press toward the dark fabric, as described in the pressing section.

6 Trim each square using the rotary cutter and a small acrylic ruler. My choice of ruler is a small 6" square with a 45-degree angle printed diagonally on the ruler. Place the diagonal of the ruler along the seam, with the fabric right side up. Trim two sides of the half-square triangle with the rotary cutter. For accuracy, be sure the diagonal corner of the ruler is on the seam line. Placing the weight of your hand near the edge of the ruler will keep the fabric from creeping as you cut.

7 Reposition the ruler on the other end of the diagonal seam, and trim the sides to the required measurement. Trim all four sides.

Another method of making half-square triangles is to mark the diagonal on the squares, and then measure and sew a line ¼" to each side of the diagonal. Cut on the diagonal. Press and trim to the desired size.

Note: If you have another method of making half-square triangles that is accurate, feel free to use it to make the half-squares the size indicated in each pattern. Many of us find trimming to size makes up for slight inaccuracies in cutting, piecing, or pressing. Use whatever method is most accurate for you.

Quarter-Square Triangles

1 Make two half-square triangles the size indicated.

2 Place the half-square triangles right sides together, alternating colors and interlocking the seams. Mark the diagonal, and sew ¼" seam on both sides of diagonal.

3 Press, cut on the diagonal, open, and press again. Carefully trim the squares, keeping the diagonal of the seam on the diagonal of a square ruler. It is necessary to trim, measuring from the **center** of the block each time, to keep the X in the center of the block.

Trimming from one side only will result in uneven quarter-square triangles. Check the corners to make sure they are properly aligned before trimming the squares on two sides. Reposition the ruler on the other side of the diagonal seam, again measuring from the center of the square, and trim the sides to the required measurement. Two triangle squares will make two quarter-square triangles.

Johanna and Henrietta's granddaughter, Marcia Miles, hold one end of Henrietta's quilt, while Karla Schulz holds the other end.

Setting Triangles

1 Cut the square(s) to the size indicated. Cut diagonally.

2 Mark the center of the bias edge on the large triangles and the center of the opposite sides on the pieced blocks. Match the centers, and sew to the opposite sides of the block as in the Diagonal Four Patch (page 60).

3 Handle the bias edges carefully, and sew the seam with the large triangle on the underside to keep from stretching the bias edge.

4 When four setting triangles are indicated, cut two large squares and follow the same procedure. Repeat with the other sides. Trim to the size indicated in the pattern directions by placing the diagonal of a square ruler along the diagonal seam.

Some quilts require Quarter-Square Triangles for setting. In this case, cut the square in half diagonally in both directions. Handle the bias edges very carefully to avoid stretching. Mark the center of the triangle side by folding it in half and finger pressing at the edge. Find the center of the blocks the same way. Match the creases, and pin in place. Stitch the pieces together with the triangle on the bottom to avoid stretching when sewing. This is the method used in the Wind Across the Hill quilts.

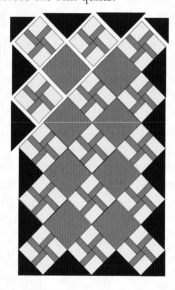

Flip Corners

Sewing along the diagonal of the small square allows you to create a triangle without cutting the fabric on the diagonal, thus avoiding possible distortion. Single, double, and double/double flip corners are used in the book projects. Each is described below.

Marking the Diagonal

There are several methods of sewing along the diagonal line. Try each and decide which way works best for you. You can chain sew all the pieces with any of these methods.

Method one: Draw a line from corner to corner with a marking pen or pencil. Hold the ruler firmly to avoid rippling. Stitch on the line.

Method two: Fold and press the diagonal of the square with wrong sides together. Place the square on the fabric to be sewn with the diagonal in the correct direction. Sew in the ditch created by the fold.

Method three: Mark a guide line on the bed of your machine with a fine permanent pen directly in front of the needle as long as possible. This method allows you to sew the diagonals without marking or folding each one. Begin sewing the diagonal with one corner of the square under the needle and the opposite corner on the line drawn with a fine permanent. Stitch the seam, guiding the opposite corner of the square along the drawn line.

To stabilize the piece, I like to trim the back of the inner triangle only, leaving the background piece as a guide for sewing the next piece. Press all the pieces flat as they come from the machine. Fold the square over the background piece, and press along the seam line. Use the method that gives you the best results.

Single Flip Corner— one triangle

Using pieces the size indicated in the pattern, sew a square on the diagonal in the direction indicated. Trim the inner triangle, press flat, fold over the background piece, and press again.

Double Flip Corner—two triangles

Using pieces the size indicated in the pattern, sew a square on the diagonal in the direction indicated.

Follow the steps for Single-Flip Corner including pressing. Sew a second square as noted in the pattern. Be sure the angle of the second square matches the illustration.

Double/Double Flip Corner—four triangles

Using pieces the size indicated in the pattern, sew a square on the diagonal in the direction indicated.

Follow the directions for Single-Flip Corner. Place a second square on the opposite corner and repeat the procedure. Trim and press. Repeat with the last two corners.

Note: *To help stabilize the pieces, I suggest trimming the inner triangle only. If your sewing deviates a bit from the diagonal, you will have the original rectangle or square visible to use as a guide for sewing to the next piece.*

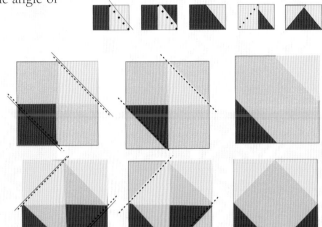

Pillow Backs

1 Cut two fabric pieces for the pillow backs, according to the directions. Fold each piece in half wrong sides together. Stitch ⅜" from the fold to secure the edge of each piece.

2 Lay one folded back on top of the other, overlapping the folded edges to equal the measurement of the pillow top. Lay the quilted pillow top right side up on the back pieces. Pin the two layers together to hold the pieces while stitching around the pieces with a scant ¼" basting stitch.

3 Complete the pillow by sewing your binding of choice around the edge. Finish as you would finish a quilt (see Finishing, page 17). Insert the appropriate pillow form or stuffing. Slip stitching the edge is optional.

Signature blocks

Method one: Press the shiny side of freezer paper to the wrong side of the block to be signed. This will stabilize the fabric for signing with a permanent fabric pen. After the blocks are signed, press with a hot iron to set the ink. Remove the freezer paper before sewing the blocks together.

Method two: If the blocks are to be signed after quilt construction, press the shiny side of a square of freezer paper to the back of each signature block. Cut the paper the scant size of the block (3½" for a 4" finished block). Use permanent fabric pens for signing. Press to set the ink. Remove the paper. Piece as usual.

Mary Martin checks the binding as Nancy Linnerooth searches for her signature on the Plum Creek banner.

... And Quilt Endings

▶Borders

A variety of borders are included in this book. The length of each border is determined after the quilt top is pieced. There is no reason to actually measure the border pieces.

Plain borders

See Sandy's quilt, page 17.

1 Carefully lay strips of border fabric lengthwise on the center of the quilt. Smooth any wrinkles. Cut two lengthwise borders.

2 Find and mark the center of the border and the quilt top. Match and pin the centers and each end of the strip. Continue pinning the strips every four to five inches.

3 Sew the lengthwise borders to the sides of the quilt. Press toward the border.

4 Lay strips of border fabric crosswise on the center of the quilt, and cut two crosswise borders.

5 Find and mark the center of the border and quilt top. Match and pin the centers and each end of the strip. Continue pinning the strips every four to five inches.

6 Sew the crosswise borders to the sides of the quilt. Press toward the border.

Borders with blocks or squares in the corners

See Wind Farm, page 29.

1 Lay strips of border fabric lengthwise on the center of the quilt. Cut to size. Set aside.

2 Lay strips of border fabric crosswise on the center of the quilt. Cut to size. Set aside.

3 Find and mark the center of the lengthwise border pieces and sides of the quilt. Match and pin the centers and each end of the strip. Continue pinning the strips every four to five inches.

4 Sew the lengthwise borders to the sides of the quilt. Press toward the border.

5 Sew blocks or squares to each end of the crosswise borders. Press toward the border.

6 Find and mark the center of the crosswise border pieces and sides of the quilt. Match and pin the seams.

7 Sew the crosswise borders in place. Press toward the border.

Side-by-Side Borders

Some quilts have border pieces that are sewn together before they are cut and sewn to the quilt, as in the Windmill quilts, page 21, and the Prairie Sampler, page 114.

Pieced Borders

Exceptions to this method occur when you have pieced blocks in the border. One example is the Feathered Cross quilt, page 102, where you are given the measurement that the previous border must be to have the pieced blocks fit properly.

Minute differences, less than ⅛", may be adjusted by placing the piece with excess fabric on the bottom when you sew the seam. Finding, marking, and pinning the center of the pieces being sewn will spread the extra fabric evenly over the length of the seam. Sewn carefully, the extra will not be visible after the seam is pressed. If an adjustment of more than ⅛" is necessary, it may be possible to "find" the extra by taking in or letting out several of the seams. Check the seams on the wrong side, and see if adjusting would improve the seam allowance. Several seams too large or too small will make a considerable difference in the final size.

▶Finishing

Quilting

Hand quilting designs may be marked on your quilt before layering. You may also use the quilt pieces for stitching guides. Test all markers before using. If you prefer to have your quilt machine stitched, seek an electric needle specialist in your area. Ask to see a sample of his or her work and for the name of a satisfied customer before leaving your quilt. If you are sending your quilt to a machine quilter, you will not need to layer the pieces.

Quilt backs

The machine quilter will tell you how much larger to prepare the back. Our backs have four inches added to the back measurements. I often use leftover pieces of fabric sewn together any way they fit for the back of the quilt. An extra block or two creates a pleasant and unexpected surprise when included on the back. It adds interest, it's color coordinated with the top, and it helps keep your stash from growing. I must warn you that it may require more time to "design" the back than you may feel it's worth. In that case, use the largest pieces available, because these will require the fewest seams.

- For quilts up to 75" long, I use one crosswise seam. Measure the quilt crosswise, add six to this number, and then double the number. Divide the total by 36 to figure the amount of fabric to purchase for the back.

- For quilts more than 75" wide and less that 75" long, I use one lengthwise seam. Measure the quilt lengthwise, add six to this number, and then double the number. Divide the total by 36 to figure the amount of fabric to purchase for the back.

- For quilts larger than 75", I use two seams. Measure the shortest side, add six to this number, and then multiple by three. Divide by 36 to figure the amount of fabric to purchase for the back.

Press the pieces and open the seams before sandwiching the quilt.

The back of Sandy's quilt is every bit as good looking as the front! Sandy made oversized blocks from the fabric left over from her Prairie Sampler to make this wonderful example of a reversible quilt. It took a long time but was worth it! Quilt by Sandy Frigo, Menomonie, Wis. Quilted by Bonnie Erickson, Granite Falls, Minn.

▶Quilt Sandwich

1 Sandwich your quilt by placing the back right side down on a flat surface. A large table will save your back. Quilt shops often have classrooms available to use. Church tables pushed together are another option. For the more agile quilter, the floor may be a possibility.

2 Secure the top edge of the quilt to the flat surface with masking tape or with clips. Lay the batting on the quilt back. Smooth out any wrinkles. Lay the quilt top over the batting, right side up, and baste in place every three to four inches. You may use safety pins, basting thread, or the new quilt-tack device. If you will be machine quilting, baste with safety pins.

3 Quilt as desired by hand or by machine.

▶Quilt Hanger

1 Cut a strip 6" wide and 1" shorter than the width of the quilt. Turn under ¼" at each short end. Turn again and stitch.

2 Fold the strip in half lengthwise, with wrong sides together. Press.

3 Machine baste the hanger to the back of the quilt, matching the raw edges of the quilt and the hanger at the top.

4 Slip stitch the folded edge of the hanger to the back of the quilt.

Note: I use a flat "screen" molding, available at lumber yards, for a hanger. It is inexpensive and can easily be cut any size you wish.

Johanna and husband/illustrator, Ormon, review illustrations for the book.

Johanna at work at her sewing machine on a winter day.

▶Binding

1 Trim the backing and batting. Baste ¼" from the outer edge of the quilt to hold the layers and keep them from slipping as the binding is applied. A walking foot makes sewing the binding easier.

Binding is usually cut crosswise across the width of the fabric. I use 2½" wide binding strips for small quilts and increase the width to 2¾" for bed quilts.

If I am using a stripe or plaid binding, I cut the pieces on the bias. Using a rotary cutter, cut the fabric at a 45-degree angle along the diagonal on a long ruler. Cut the width as desired on the bias edge. Cut enough strips to equal the length indicated in the pattern.

2 Sew the binding strips right sides together at right angles to create the length indicated in the pattern. Fold the binding strip in half lengthwise with wrong sides together. Press.

3 Pin the binding to the right side of one side of the quilt every four to five inches, matching the edges and leaving a 10" tail un-sewn.

4 Sew to ¼" of the first corner. Remove the quilt from the machine. Miter the corners by folding the binding at right angles perpendicular to the direction of the sewn seam. Refold the binding back on itself so the second fold is even with the edge of the side of the quilt.

5 Pin and sew the binding to the next corner and repeat miter-ing the corners until all sides are sewn, leaving a second 10" tail unsewn.

6 Overlap the binding edges and cut one end longer than the other, exactly the width of the cut binding. With the quilt toward you, open the binding and place the right end of the binding over the left end, right sides together at right angles. Pin. Sew on the diagonal, corner to corner. Check to see that the seam is correct, trim the seam, press, and complete sewing on the binding.

7 Turn the folded edge of the binding to the back of the quilt, covering the stitching line, and slip stitch in place with thread to match the binding.

8 Admire your quilt.

▶Sign and date your quilt

Use a permanent marking fabric pen to sign the quilt back, or create a personal label for the quilt.

1 To make a label, stabilize it by pressing the shiny side of freezer paper to the back of the label fabric.

2 Write your name, address, date, and other pertinent information about the quilt on the label with permanent fabric pens. Embellish as you wish.

3 Press to set the ink. Remove the freezer paper, turn under the edges, and hand stitch the label to the quilt. Imagine the pleasure someone will have in the future when he or she finds one of your signed quilts in a trunk!

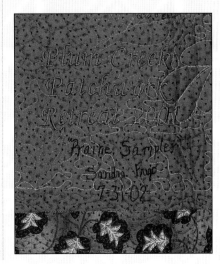

Time to dream about beginning another quilt.

Block Box #1

Windmill

piecing

Please, review Strip Piecing (page 12). These directions will explain how to make the four-block section used in the Prairie Sampler.

1 Sew a 2½" background strip and 1½" accent strip together on the long side. Press toward the accent strip. Cut at 3½" intervals. Make four cuts for each block.

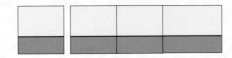

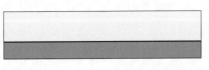

2 Sew the cut pieces from step 1 together in pairs, repositioning the pieces as shown.

3 Sew the pairs together to make each block (6½" x 6½").

4 Make and sew four blocks together for the sampler (6½" x 24½").

5 Set aside for the sampler quilt.

cutting

- From background cut:
  4 strips, 2½" x 16"
- From accent fabric cut:
  4 strips, 1½" x 16"

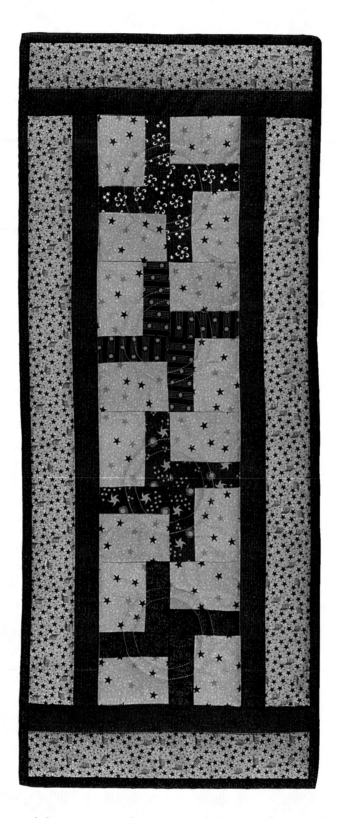

This table runner is a quick colorful quilt
project suitable for beginners, as a last
minute gift, or for a change of season.

Summer Wind Table Runner

Linda Brandt, Anamosa, Ia.
Karla Schulz, Jackson, Minn.

blocks

Piece four Windmill blocks (6½" x 24½").

construction

Please, review Borders, page 16.

1 Sew an outer border piece to each inner border piece on the long sides. Press toward the inner border.

2 Measure the length of the Windmill blocks through the middle. Cut two border pieces this size. Sew one to each long side of the quilt. Press toward the inner border.

3 Measure the width of the top through the middle. Cut two border pieces this size.

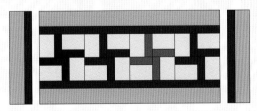

size: 12" x 30"

additional materials

- ⅛ yard inner border fabric cut into:
  2 strips, 1½" x 42"
- ¼ yard outer border fabric cut into:
  2 strips, 2½" x 42"
- Backing fabric, ¾ yard
- Batting, 16" x 34"
- ¼ yard binding fabric cut into:
  3 binding strips, 2½" wide

finishing, see page 17

1 Sandwich, quilt, and then bind your quilt with 2½" wide binding strips pieced to measure 100".

2 Sign and date your quilt.

Note: *To adjust the size of the table runner, change the number of blocks.*

Wind across the Hill is a gift made by the participants of the first Plum Creek Quilt Retreat. Each quilter made a Windmill block from scraps left from their Prairie Sampler. The quilt was then pieced by Karla Schulz, quilted by Bonnie Erickson, and presented to Margaret Yackel-Juleen at Shalom Hill Farm as a thank you for a wonderful retreat. The label on the back of the quilt includes the signature and hometown of each quilter.

Wind across the Hill

Johanna Wilson, Walnut Grove, Minn.
Quilted by Bonnie Erickson, Granite Falls, Minn.

materials

	Wall Quilt	Twin Quilt	Queen Quilt
Finished Size	41½" x 58½"	62½" x 80"	92" x 92"
Background—Light Blocks	¾ yard	1½ yards	2¼ yards
Background—Medium Blocks	½ yard	⅞ yard	2¼ yards
Background—Dark Framing Triangles	⅓ yard	½ yard	¾ yard
Scraps for Windmills	⅓ yard	¾ yard	1½ yards
Border #1	⅓ yard	½ yard	¾ yard
Border #2	1 yard	2⅝ yards	2¾ yards
Backing	2¾ yards	4 yards	8½ yards
Batting	44" x 62"	66" x 84"	96" x 96"
Binding	½ yard	⅝ yard	⅞ yard

size:

Wall Quilt:
41½" x 58½"

Twin Quilt:
62½" x 80"

Queen Quilt:
92" x 92"

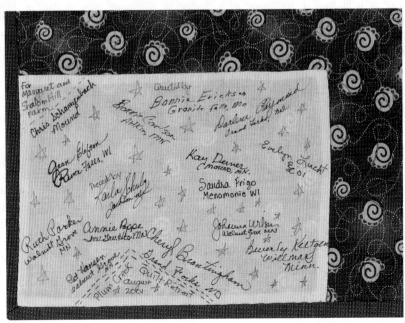

Each quilter signed the back of the Wind across the Hill quilt.

cutting for the Wind across the Hill wall quilt

	Number of Strips	Size to cut strips WOF	Number of Pieces	Size of Pieces
Background—Light	8	2½"	15	2½" x 15"
Background—Medium	2	6½"	8	6½" x 6½"
Background—Dark	1	10"	3	10" x 10"
	1	7"	2	7" x 7"
Accent or Scraps			15	1½" x 15"
Border #1	4	2½"		
Border #2	4	6½"		
Binding	5	2½"		

cutting for the Wind across the Hill twin quilt

	Number of Strips	Size to cut strips WOF	Number of Pieces	Size of Pieces
Background—Light	19	2½"	35	2½" x 15"
Background—Medium	4	6½"	24	6½" x 6½"
Background—Dark	2	10"	5	10" x 10"
			2	7" x 7"
Accent or Scraps			35	1½" x 15"
Border #1	6	2½"		
Border #2	6	8½"		
Binding	8	2¾"		

cutting for the Wind across the Hill queen quilt

	Number of Strips	Size to cut strips WOF	Number of Pieces	Size of Pieces
Background—Light	11	2½"	64	2½" x 15"
Background—Medium	8	6½"	49	6½" x 6½"
Background—Dark	1	10"	4	10" x 10"
	1	7"	3	7" x 7"
Accent or Scraps			64	1½" x 15"
Border #1	8	2½"		
Border #2	9	10½"		
Binding	10	2¾"		

piecing

Make the number of Windmill blocks indicated for the desired size quilt.

Wind across the Hill	Wall Quilt	Twin Quilt	Queen Quilt
Number of blocks	15	35	64

quilt construction

Directions are for the wall quilt. Bed quilt changes are in parentheses (twin, queen).

1 Arrange and then sew 15 (35, 64) pieced blocks and 8 (24, 49) medium background squares in diagonal rows.

2 Cut the 10" dark background squares diagonally twice for a total of 12 triangles.

3 Arrange and then sew the large dark background triangles to the ends of each row. Handle the bias edges of the triangles carefully. ***Note:*** *Line the large triangles up at the edge of the pieced blocks so they extend beyond the outside edge. Triangles will be trimmed after Step 6.*

4 Press the seams in all rows toward the background blocks. ***Note:*** *Pressing the rows in opposite directions will interlock the intersections of the blocks as the rows are sewn together.*

5 Cut the 7" dark background squares diagonally once for a total of 14 triangles.

6 Center the smaller triangles on the corner blocks. ***Note:*** *To find the center of the triangles, carefully fold them in half along the bias edge and finger press at the edge. Finger press the center of the block. Match the centers, and sew with the triangle on the bottom. Press toward the triangle.*

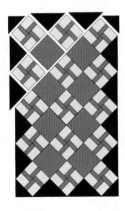

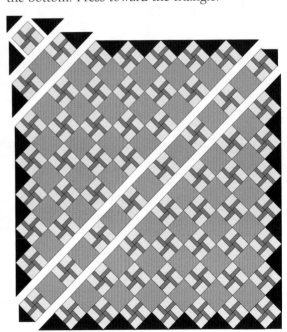

7 Sew the rows together. Trim the outer triangles ¼" beyond the edges of the pieced blocks.

borders, see page 16

1 Sew Border #1 and Border #2 pieces side by side. Press toward Border #1.

2 Measure and cut two borders the length of the quilt top. Sew them to the sides of the quilt. Press toward Border #1.

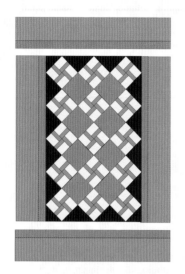

3 Measure and cut two borders the width of the quilt. Sew them to the top and bottom of the quilt. Press toward Border #1.

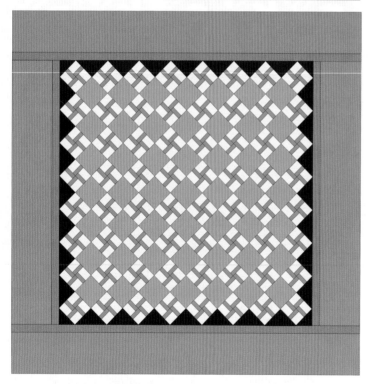

finishing, see page 17

1 Sandwich, quilt, and then bind your quilt with 2½" (2¾", 2¾") wide binding strips pieced to measure 210" (300", 420").

2 Sign and date your quilt.

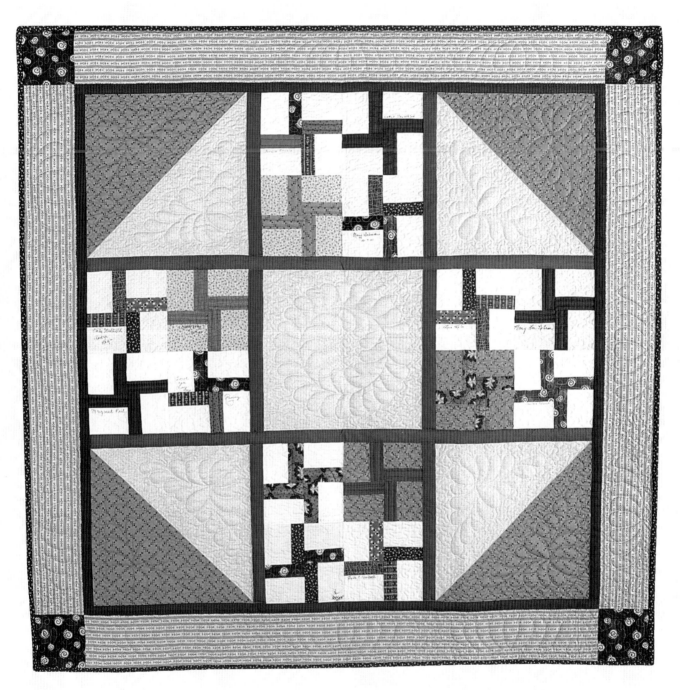

This quilt was made with leftover scraps from a retreat in Wisconsin. Each quilter signed their block. The large setting blocks offer an opportunity for the quilter to add fancy stitches.

Wind Farm

Johanna Wilson, Walnut Grove, Minn.
Quilted by Bonnie Erickson, Granite Falls, Minn.

size:

Wall Quilt:
48" x 48"

Queen Quilt:
102" x 102"

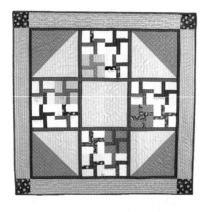

materials

	Wall Quilt	Queen Quilt
Finished Size	48" x 48"	102" x 102"
Background—Assorted Lights for Blocks, Setting Square and Triangles	1 yard	3¾ yards
Background—Medium	½ yard	1¼ yards
Scraps for Windmills and Corner Squares	½ yard	1¾ yards
Sashing for Blocks	¼ yard	¾ yard
Border #1	¼ yard	¾ yard
Border #2	1¼ yard lengthwise stripe or ⅝ yard cut crosswise	1¾ yards cut crosswise
Border #3		2 yards
Batting	52" x 52"	106" x 106"
Backing	3 yards	9 yards
Binding	½ yard	1 yard

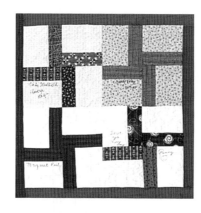

cutting for the Wind Farm wall quilt

	Number of Strips	Size to cut strips WOF	Number of Pieces	Size of Pieces
Background—Assorted Lights				
Blocks	1	2½"	16	2½" x 15"
Large Triangles		13"	2	13" x 13"
Setting Square			1	12½" x 12½"
Background—Medium				
Large Triangles	1	13"	2	13" x 13"
Scraps for Blocks		1½"	16	1½" x 15"
and Corner Stones	1		9	4½" x 4½"
Sashing for Blocks	4	1½"	2	1½" x 38½"
			6	1½" x 12½"
Border #1	4	1¼"	2	1¼" x 38½"
			2	1¼" x 40½"
Border #2	4	4½" cut lengthwise		
Binding	5	2½"		

cutting for the Wind Farm queen quilt

	Number of Strips	Size to cut strips WOF	Number of Pieces	Size of Pieces
Background—Assorted		2½"	64	2½" x 15"
Lights for Blocks, Setting				
Square and Triangles	4	13"	8	13" x 13"
			4	12½" x 12½"
Background—Medium	3	13"	8	13" x 13"
Scraps for Blocks and				
Corner Stones		1½"	64	1½" x 15"
	1	6½"	4	6½" x 6½"
	1	4½"	9	4½" x 4½"
Sashing for Blocks	16	1½"	8	1½" x 38½"
			24	1½" x 12½"
Block Border #1	16	1¼"	8	1¼" x 38½"
			8	1¼" x 40½"
Border #2/Quilt Sashing	12	4½"	12	4½" x 40½"
Border #3	9	6½"		
Binding	11	2¾"		

piecing

Make the number of Windmill blocks indicated for the desired size quilt.

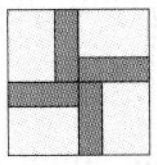

Wind Farm	Wall Quilt	Queen Quilt
Number of blocks	16	64

Wall Quilt

quilt construction

Directions are for the wall quilt. Queen quilt changes are in parentheses (queen).

1 Piece four windmill blocks together to make a 12½" block. Arrange the signatures and the scraps in a pleasing manner.

2 Make half-square triangles from 13" light and medium background squares. Trim each square to 12½". Make 4 (16).

3 Arrange large half-square triangles and Windmill blocks in rows. Sew 1½" sashing strips to both sides of the center blocks. Press toward the sashing.

4 Sew rows of blocks together. Press toward the sashing.

5 Sew 1½" sashing to the top and bottom of the center row. Press toward the sashing.

6 Sew the three rows together (38½" x 38½"). Make 1 (4).

7 Sew 1½" Border #1 pieces to the sides and then to the top and bottom of the blocks (40½" X 40½"). Make 1 (4)

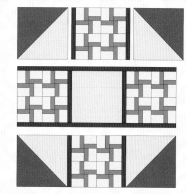

borders, see page 16

1 Measure and cut two Border #2 pieces 4½" wide by the length of the quilt and two Border #2 pieces 4½" wide by the width of quilt.

2 Sew the borders to opposite sides of the quilt. Press toward the border.

3 Sew the corner squares to each end of the remaining borders. Press toward the border.

4 Sew the borders to the top and the bottom of the quilt. Press toward the borders.

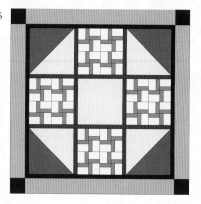

finishing, see page 17

1 Sandwich, quilt, and then bind your quilt with 2½" wide binding strips pieced to measure 210".

2 Sign and date your quilt.

Queen Quilt

1 Follow Wall Quilt steps 1 to 7.

2 Arrange the four 40½" blocks and the quilt sashing in two rows. Sew the sashing between the pairs of blocks.

3 Sew a 4½" square between two quilt sashings. Make three. Sew one set between the rows of blocks and one set to each side of the quilt.

4 Sew three squares and two quilt sashings together, beginning and ending with the squares.

5 Sew one border to the top and one to the bottom of the quilt.

6 Measure and cut two outer Border #3 pieces each the length and the width of the quilt.

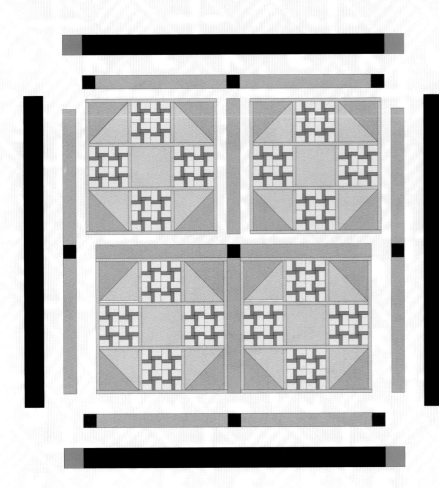

7 Sew one lengthwise piece to each side of the quilt. Sew a square to each end of the remaining crosswise pieces. Sew the crosswise pieces to the top and the bottom of the quilt.

finishing, see page 17

1 Sandwich, quilt, and then bind your quilt with 2¾" wide binding strips pieced to measure 420".

2 Sign and date your quilt.

Block Box #2
Tree

Please, review Half Square Triangles, page 12. Directions are for one block. Make the number of blocks indicated for your size quilt.

1 Make 14 half-square triangles from assorted backgrounds and darks. Trim to 4½" x 4½".

2 Arrange and sew the triangles in two columns. The columns will be sewn together in Step 5.

3 Sew the trunk fabric rectangle to the side of the 3" x 5½" background rectangle. Press toward the trunk fabric. Sew to the bottom of the left column of half squares.

4 Sew the 2½" x 4½" background rectangle to the top of the right column and the 3½" x 4½" rectangle to the bottom of the right column. Press.

5 Sew the two columns together.

6 Set aside for the Sampler quilt.

- From assorted backgrounds cut:
  - 7 squares, 5" x 5"
  - 1 rectangle, 2½" x 4½"
  - 1 rectangle, 3½" x 4½"
  - 1 rectangle, 3" x 5½"
- From trunk fabric cut:
  - 1 rectangle 2" x 5½
- From assorted darks for the tree cut:
  - 7 squares, 5" x 5"

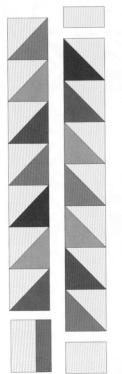

Quilts are born out of necessity and often prompted by fabric collections. A tall narrow space needed a quilt and that along with a growing collection of blue batiks made the combination that led to the creation of this quilt. It's namesake, a majestic Blue Spruce, stands as sentry visible out the window at night. Overhead stars can be seen in the distance on a clear night. Star fabric was used for the top border.

Night Watch wall quilt

Johanna Wilson, Walnut Grove, Minn.

cutting

	Number of Strips	Size to cut strips WOF	Number of Pieces	Size of Pieces
Assorted Darks*			7	5" x 5"
Assorted Lights			7	5" x 5"
			1	2½" x 4½"
			1	3½" x 4½"
			1	3" x 5½"
Trunk Fabric	Scraps		1	2" x 5½"
Border	2	2½"		
Binding	3	2½"		

* The tree has seven half-square triangles on each side.

size: 12" x 37"

materials

- Assorted darks to equal to ¼ yard
- Assorted lights to equal to ⅜ yard
- Trunk fabric scraps
- Border fabric, ¼ yard
- Backing fabric, ½ yard
- Batting, 16" x 41"
- Binding, ¼ yard

piecing

Make one Tree block using 14 half-square triangles trimmed to 4½" x 4½".

borders, see page 16

1 Measure and cut two borders the length of the tree. Sew them to the sides of the Tree block. Press toward the border.

2 Measure and cut two borders the width of the quilt. Sew them to the top and bottom of the tree block. Press toward the border.

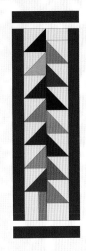

finishing, see page 17

1 Sandwich, quilt, and then bind your quilt with 2½" wide binding strips pieced to measure 110".

2 Sign and date your quilt.

Bonnie Carlson, a participant in the first Plum Creek Quilt Retreat, wanted to make her Prairie Sampler quilt larger. One option was to enlarge the quilt with borders. Another was to make a separate quilt to cover the pillows. Bonnie designed the Pillow Quilt to meet her size requirements. The trees have four half-square triangles on each side. If you have a special size requirement, adjust the number of triangle squares to make the tree the height you need. You can also make adjustments to the width of the sashing and borders. Be creative!

Note: Bonnie alternated the sides of the trunks and the backgrounds of the trees for variety.

cutting

	Number of Strips	Size to cut strips WOF	Number of Pieces	Size of Pieces
Assorted Greens*			36	5" x 5"
Light Background	3	5"	20	5" x 5"
	1	4½"	5	2½" x 4½"
			5	3½" x 4½"
	1	3"	5	3" x 5½"
Dark Background	2	5"	16	5" x 5"
	1	4½"	4	2½" x 4½"
			4	3½" x 4½"
	1	3"	4	3" x 5½"
Assorted Trunk Fabric			8	2" x 5½"
Sashing	5	2"	8	2" x 21½"
Border #1	5	2½"		
Border #2	6	2½"		
Binding	6	2½"		

*Each tree has four half-square triangles on each side

Tree Top pillow quilt

Bonnie Carlson, Aiken, Minn.
Quilted by Bonnie Erickson, Granite Falls, Minn.

piecing

Make nine Tree blocks using 72 half-square triangles, eight for each tree. Trim half-square triangles to 4½" x 4½".

size: 27" x 90"

quilt construction

1. Make five tree blocks with light backgrounds and trunks on the left side of the tree.
2. Make four tree blocks with dark backgrounds and trunks on the right side of the tree.
3. Sew sashing to the right hand side of eight trees, four with light backgrounds and four with dark backgrounds. Press toward the sashing.
4. Sew nine trees side by side, alternating light and dark backgrounds. Press toward the sashing.

materials

- Assorted darks to equal 1½ yards
- Assorted lights to equal ¾ yard
- Trunk fabric scraps
- Sashing, ⅜ yard
- Border fabric #1, ½ yard
- Border fabric #2, ½ yard
- Backing, 2 yards
- Batting, 31" x 94"
- Binding, ½ yard

borders, see page 16

1. Measure and cut two borders the length at the center of the quilt. Sew them to the sides of the quilt.
2. Measure and piece two borders the width at the center of the quilt. Sew them to the top and bottom of the quilt.
3. Repeat with the outer border.

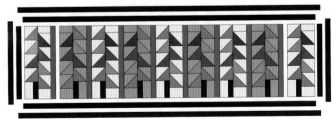

finishing, see page 17

1. Sandwich, quilt, and then bind your quilt with 2½" wide binding strips pieced to measure 260".
2. Sign and date your quilt.

Block Box #3

Four Patch— Broken Dishes

piecing

Please, review Strip Piecing, page 12, and Half-Square Triangles, page 12. Directions are for three Four Patch blocks and two Broken Dishes blocks. Make the number of blocks indicated for your size quilt.

cutting

- From background cut:
  1 strip, 2½" x 16"
  4 squares, 3" x 3"
- From light fabric cut:
  1 strip, 2½" x 16"
- From medium fabric cut:
  4 squares, 3" x 3"

four patch

1 Sew 2½" strips of background fabric and light fabric together along the long edge. Press toward the darker fabric.

2 Cut at 2½" intervals. Make six cuts.

3 Sew in pairs alternating colors. Make three (4½" x 4½").

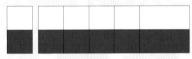

broken dishes

1 Make eight half-square triangles from 3" squares (2½" x 2½").

2 Sew the half squares together in pairs, alternating colors (2½" x 4½").

3 Sew the pairs together. Make two Broken Dishes blocks (4½" x 4½").

quilt construction

1 Sew the three Four Patch blocks and the two Broken Dishes blocks together, beginning and ending with a Four Patch block.

2 Set aside for the Sampler quilt.

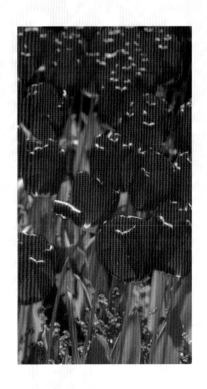

Quilters combine two blocks in a quilt for the variety of designs that can be created. The combination of the basic Four Patch and a variation, Broken Dishes, makes an interesting frame for a small quilt or pillow. The center of the Redwork Flag quilt and the Bluework Pillow quilt are interchangeable.

Redwork Flag

Johanna Wilson, Walnut Grove, Minn.

cutting

	Number of Strips	Size to cut strips WOF	Number of Pieces	Size of Pieces
Background—light	1		1	13" x 13"
			16	3" x 3"
	1	2½"		
Blue—Blocks	1	2½"		
Red—Blocks	2	3"	16	3" x 3"
Binding	2	2½"		

size: 20" x 20"

materials

- Background for blocks, ½ yard
- Blue fabric for blocks, ½ yard
- Red fabric for blocks, ½ yard
- Backing, 24" x 24"
- Batting, 24" x 24"
- Binding, ½ yard
- #8 pearl cotton red and/or blue
- #7 embroidery needle
- Fine red marking pen
- Small hoop (optional)

background

1 Trace the flag design, page 44, onto the 13" square with a fine red marking pen. You won't need to remove the lines, as they will be covered by your stitches. **Note:** *To center the flag on the fabric, fold the square in half twice to make four quadrants. Crease lightly. Match the center creases with the lines on the center of the flag.*

Stem stitch

1 Imagine letters in this order A C B D.

2 Bring your needle up from bottom at A, down at B, up at C and down at D. Continue in this manner while holding the thread to the left of the stitches as you work.

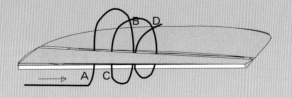

2 Embroider the flag with a stem stitch or a small running stitch. A small hoop is helpful to keep the fabric taut while you stitch.

3 Press very gently face down on a towel. Trim the square to measure 12½".

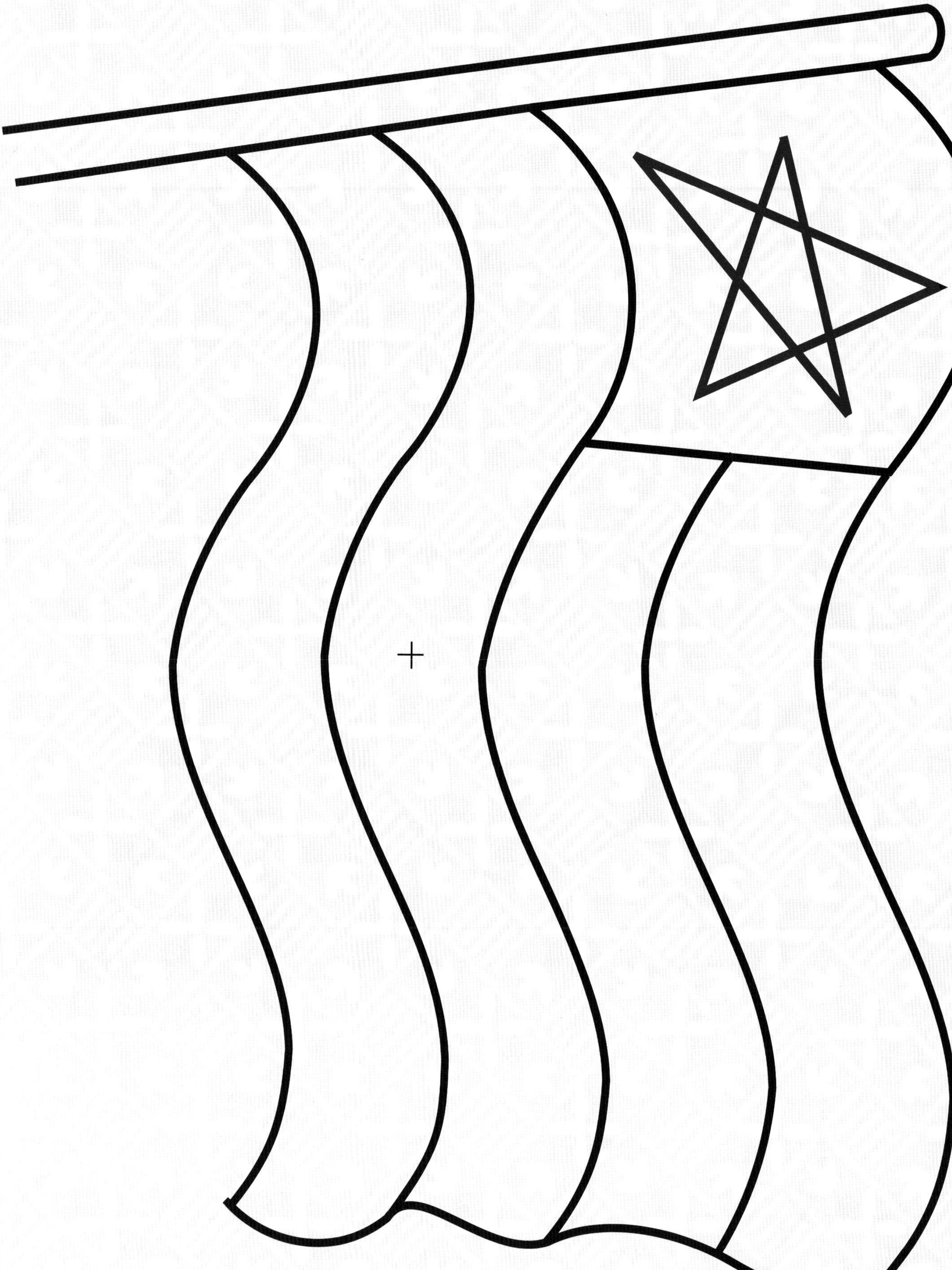

four patch

Please, review Strip Piecing, page 12.

1 Sew 2½" strips of background fabric and blue fabric together along the long edge. Press toward the darker fabric.

2 Cut at 2½" intervals. Make 16 cuts.

3 Sew two pairs together, alternating fabrics. Make eight Four Patch blocks (4½" x 4½").

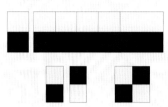

broken dishes

Please, review Half-Square Triangles, page 12.

1 Make 32 half-square triangles from 3" background squares and red squares (2½" x 2½").

2 Sew the half-square triangles in pairs, alternating color and direction. Make 16 (2½" x 4½").

3 Sew pairs together. Make eight Broken Dishes blocks (4½" x 4½").

border blocks

1 Sew two Four Patch blocks and one Broken Dishes block together, beginning and ending with a Four Patch block. Make two border pieces (4½" x 12½"). ***Note:*** *All the blocks "point" in the direction of the upper right corner.*

2 Sew the borders to the sides of the center square. Press toward the center.

3 Sew three Broken Dishes blocks and two Four Patch blocks together, beginning and ending with a Broken Dishes block. Make two (20½" x 4½").

4 Sew border blocks to the top and bottom of the quilt. Press toward the center.

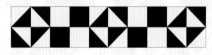

finishing, see page 17

1 Sandwich, quilt, and then bind your quilt with 2½" wide binding strips pieced to measure 90". Quilting between the lines of the red stripes adds dimension to the flag. Additional quilting stitches surround the entire flag.

2 Sign and date your quilt.

Our quilt uses two shades of blue. You may prefer to use only one shade for your quilt or many shades for a scrappy look. This project also lends itself to a hand-quilted center, using colored or neutral quilting thread. Several more parallel lines inside the design will give the appearance of ripples, often called echo stitching.

Bluework Pillow

Johanna Wilson, Walnut Grove, Minn.

cutting

	Number of Strips	Size to cut strips WOF	Number of Pieces	Size of Pieces
Background—Light	1		1	13" x 13"
		3"	16	3" x 3"
	1	2½"		
Blue—Broken dishes	1	3"	16	3" x 3"
Blue—Four patch	1	2½"		
Binding	2	2½"		
Backing	2 lengthwise	21½" x 27"		

size: 20" x 20"

materials

- Background for blocks, ½ yard
- Blue fabric for blocks, ⅓ yard
- Backing, ¾ yard
- Batting, 24" x 24"
- Binding, ¼ yard
- #8 pearl cotton red and/or blue
- #7 embroidery needle
- Fine blue marking pen
- Small hoop (optional)

making a template

1 Trace the template, page 49, on paper, marking the fold lines as indicated by the dotted lines. Cut out carefully. Set aside.

2 Fold the 13" background square in half twice to make four quadrants. Press the fold lines. Open with right side up.

3 Place the dotted lines of the template so they are on fold lines.

4 Draw around the template with a fine blue marking pen. Do not trace the dotted lines.

5 Reposition the paper template and repeat in each quadrant. See Stem Stitch, page 45.

four patch

1 Sew 2½" strips of background fabric and blue fabric together along the long edge. Press toward the darker fabric.

2 Cut at 2½" intervals. Make 16 cuts.

3 Sew two pairs together, alternating fabrics. Make eight four patch blocks (4½" x 4½").

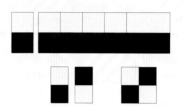

broken dishes

1 Make 32 half squares from 3" squares (2½" x 2½"). Sew two together. Make 16 (2½" x 4½").

2 Sew the half squares together in pairs, alternating color and direction. Make 16 pairs (2½" x 4½").

3 Sew the pairs together. Make eight Broken Dishes blocks (4½" x 4½").

border blocks

1 Sew two Four Patch blocks and one Broken Dishes block together, beginning and ending with a Four Patch block. Make two border pieces (4½" x 12½"). *Note: All the blocks "point" in the direction of the upper right corner.*

2 Sew the border pieces to the sides of the center square. Press toward the center.

3 Sew three Broken Dishes and two Four Patch blocks together, beginning and ending with a Broken Dishes block. Make two border pieces (20½" x 4½").

4 Sew the border pieces to the top and bottom of the quilt. Press toward the center (20½" x 20½").

finishing, see page 17

1 Sandwich, quilt, and then bind your quilt with 2½" wide binding strips pieced to measure 90".

2 Sign and date your quilt.

Our sample quilts are color
controlled. Imagine how these
projects would look from scraps
of your favorite quilt projects.
Perhaps you have a collection of
half squares just waiting to be
made into a small quilt.

Table Runner and Placemats

Johanna Wilson, Walnut Grove, Minn.
Quilted by Brenda Lee, Madison, SD.

size:

12" x 36", 12" x 18"

materials

- Background for blocks, ⅓ yard
- Centers for Table Runner and Placemats, ¾ yard
- Red print, ⅓ yard
- Backing, 1 yard
- Batting, ¾ yard
- Navy accent and binding, ½ yard
- #8 pearl cotton red and/or blue
- #7 embroidery needle
- Permanent marking pens (optional)

cutting for two placemats and a table runner

	Number of Strips	Size to cut strips WOF	Number of Pieces	Size of Pieces
Background—Light	3	3"	36	3" x 3"
Centers	2	12½"	1	12½" x 18½"
			2	12½" x 14½"
Red Print	3	3"	36	3" x 3"
Navy Accent	2	1½"	4	1½" x 12½"
Binding	6	2½"		
Backing	2	15" x 20"		
	1	15" x 40"		
Batting	2	15" x 20"		
	1	15" x 40"		
Binding	6	2½"		

quilt construction

1 Sew an accent strip to one end of each placemat rectangle and both ends of the table runner rectangle.

2 Make 18 Broken Dishes blocks (4½" x 4½"). Sew three blocks in a row. Make six rows (4½" x 12½").

3 Sew one row of blocks to one end of each placemat center.

4 Sew a double row of blocks to both ends of the table runner center.

finishing

1 Sandwich, quilt, and then bind your quilts with 2½" wide binding strips pieced to measure 250".

2 Sign and date your quilt.

Block Box #4
Pinwheels

piecing		cutting

Please, review Half-Square Triangles, page 12. Directions are for four blocks. Make the number of blocks indicated for your size quilt.

- From medium background fabric cut:
  4 squares 3" x 3"
- From 2 shades of one color cut:
  2 squares in each shade, 3" x 3"

1 Make 16 half-square triangles using the background squares and colored squares (2½" x 2½").

2 Sew the half-square triangles together in pairs. Make eight (2½" x 4½").

3 Sew the pairs together. Make four (4½" x 4½").

4 Sew the blocks together.

5 Set aside for the Prairie Sampler.

This small project in school colors is a good
choice for the graduate.

School Colors Pillow

Johanna Wilson, Walnut Grove, Minn.
Quilted by Brenda Lee, Madison, SD.

blocks

size: 18" x 18"

Piece five Pinwheel blocks.

cutting

additional materials

	Number of Strips	Size to cut strips WOF	Number of Pieces	Size of Pieces
Background				
Blocks	1	$4\frac{1}{2}$"	4	$4\frac{1}{2}$" x $4\frac{1}{2}$"
	1	3"	10	3" x 3"
Sashing			2	$1\frac{1}{4}$" x $12\frac{1}{2}$"
			2	$1\frac{1}{4}$" x 14"
Pinwheel	1	3"	10	3" x 3"
Border	2	$2\frac{3}{4}$"	4	$2\frac{3}{4}$" x $13\frac{1}{2}$"
Pillow Back	1	19"	2	19" x 21"
Binding	2	$2\frac{1}{2}$"		

- Background fabric for blocks and center, $\frac{1}{3}$ yard
- Pinwheel scraps to equal $\frac{1}{3}$ yard
- Backing, 19" x 42"
- Batting, 20" x 20"
- Binding, $\frac{1}{4}$ yard

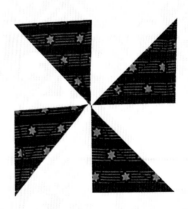

piecing

Please, review Half-Square Triangles, page 12.

1 Sew the Pinwheel blocks and 4½" background squares together in rows.

2 Sew the rows together.

3 Sew the sashing strips to the sides and then to the top and bottom of the blocks.

4 Sew two borders to opposite sides of the quilt. Sew a background square to both ends of the remaining borders. Sew to the top and bottom of the quilt.

pillow backs, see page 15

1 Cut two pillow backs, 19" x 20½". Fold the pillow backs in half, wrong sides together, to measure 19" x 10¼". Stitch ⅜" from each fold.

2 Overlap the backs at the folded edge. Lay the pillow top on the backs with the right side up.

3 Baste the edges for ease in attaching the binding.

finishing, see page 17

1 Bind your pillow with 2½" wide binding strips pieced to measure 80".

2 Sign and date your pillow.

Doll Quilt

Edie Pearson, Grand Marsh, Wis.

A perfect gift for any doll lover.

blocks

Piece four Pinwheel blocks.

finishing, see page 17

1 Sew a 4½" strip to each side of the row of pinwheel blocks (12½" x 16½").

2 Sandwich, quilt, and then bind your quilt with 2½" wide binding strips pieced to measure 80".

3 Sign and date your quilt. Give the quilt to your favorite doll lover.

materials for borders

Please, review Borders, page 16.

• Two sashing pieces, 4½" x 16½"

• Two binding strips, 2½" x 42"

This banner celebrates our new book. By changing the center message you can commemorate a graduation, special birthday, or any other important occasion. Have the guests sign the blocks ahead of time for a surprise, or at the time of the party in place of a guest book. Galen, Karla's son, painted the center of our banner using an airbrush and retreat participants signed the blocks.

Celebration Banner

Galen McCarthy, Jackson, Minn.
Karla Schulz, Jackson, Minn.

cutting

	Number of Strips	Size to cut strips WOF	Number of Pieces	Size of Pieces
Background				
Center	1	12½"	1	12½" x 20½"
Blocks			24	4½" x 4½"
			48	3" x 3"
Pinwheels	Scraps to equal 2 (80")	3"	48	3" x 3"
Backing	1	19"		
Binding	4	2¾"		

size: 28" x 36"

additional materials

- Background blocks and center, 1 yard
- Pinwheels scraps to equal ⅓ yard
- Backing, 1⅓ yards
- Batting, ¾ yard
- Binding, ⅓ yard

blocks

Piece 24 Pinwheel blocks.

piecing

1 Sew the Pinwheel blocks and 4½" background squares together in rows.

2 Sew the short rows to the sides and long strips to the top and bottom of the banner.

3 The center lettering may be done with permanent marking pen, hand or machine embroidery, or straight stitching. *Note: Alternating plain blocks may be used as signature blocks. The completed quilt top may be signed after construction. See Signature Blocks, page 15.*

Another pinwheel quilt, Summer Delight, may be found on page 112.

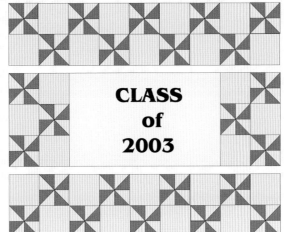

CLASS
of
2003

Clare Anderson
Mequon, WI

Sandra Frigo
Menomonie WI

Block Box #5

Diagonal Four Patch

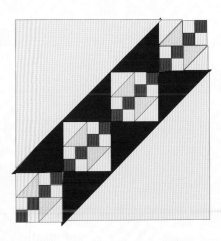

piecing—four patch

Please, review Strip Piecing, page 12, and Half-Square Triangles, page 12. Directions are for one 16½" block. Make the number of blocks indicated for your size quilt.

1 Sew a background strip and an accent strip together on the long edge. Press.

2 Cut at 1½" intervals. Make 16 cuts. Sew two cuts together, alternating colors. Make eight (2½" x 2½").

piecing—half-square triangles

1 Make eight half-square triangles from pairs of 3" squares (2½" x 2½").

2 Sew a four patch and a half square together. Press. Make eight (2½" x 4½").

3 Sew two pairs together to make a larger four patch. Press. Make four (4½" x 4½").

4 Arrange the blocks and triangles in rows, lining up the edges. You will have two extra triangles to add to your scrap bag. Sew the rows together.
Note: The long side of the tri-angles will extend beyond the squares.

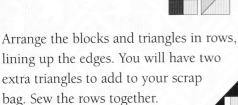

cutting

• From medium background fabric cut:
    4 squares, 3" x 3"
    1 square, 14" x 14", cut diagonally once
    2 strips, 1½" x 22"
• From accent fabric cut:
    2 strips, 1½" x 22"
    2 squares, 7½" x 7½", cut diagonally twice
• From background C cut:
    4 squares, 3" x 3"

piecing

5 Place a 24" ruler line along the diagonal so that the edge of the ruler extends ¼ " beyond the edge of the half square block. Trim.

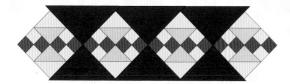

6 Carefully mark and match the center of the long edge of the large triangle and the center of the row of blocks. Sew the pieces together with the large triangle on the bottom. **Note:** *Sew with the triangle on the bottom to help keep the bias edge from stretching. Always handle bias edges with care.*

7 Press the block gently. Square the block by placing the diagonal of a large square ruler on the diagonal of the four patches. Trim the square to 16½".

8 Set aside for the Prairie Sampler.

Note: The large setting triangles offer an opportunity to showcase a special fabric, fancy stitching, or an appliqué design. Stitching may be done by hand or by machine.

Fancy machine stitching by Bonnie Erickson.

Appliqué by Kay Derner. Flowers were cut from leaf fabric and positioned to create flower petals.

Reversing the angle of the Four Patch block makes an
attractive pair of pillow covers.

Village Square pillow

Karla Schulz, Jackson, Minn.

blocks

Piece one Diagonal Four Patch block for each pillow.

additional materials

- 2 border strips, 3" x 16½"
- 2 border strips, 6" x 21½"
- 2 pillow backs, 20½" x 29"

piecing

1 Sew the 3" x 16½" border strips to the top and bottom of the block.

2 Sew the 6" x 21½" border strips to the sides of the block (20½" x 28½").

3 Quilt as desired.

4 Fold each pillow-back in half wrong sides together to measure 20½" x 14½". Stitch each ⅜" from the fold.

5 Overlap the folded backs to measure 28½". Lay the pillow top right side up over the backs and machine or pin baste together.

6 Bind with 2¾" binding strips sewn together to measure 120".

7 Slip the quilt over a standard bed pillow.

Diagonal lines can create interest in your quilt. A new design emerges when you rotate four blocks. The center is a great place for fancy stitching or appliqué. Or, use it as a lovely display area for the center of a table.

cutting

	Number of Strips	Size to cut strips WOF	Number of Pieces	Size of Pieces
Background—Light				
Setting Triangles	2	13¾"	4	13¾" x 13¾"
Blocks	3	1½"		
	1	3"	16	3" x 3"
Accent or Scraps for Blocks				
	3	1½"		
Border Squares	1	3"	16	3" x 3"
	1	6"	4	6" x 6"
Diagonal Triangles	2	7½"	6	7½" x 7½"
Border #1	4	1½"	2	1½" x 32½"
			2	1½" x 34½"
Border #2	4	6"	4	6" x 34½"
Backing	1	44" x 44"		
Batting		44" x 44"		
Binding	5	2¾"		

Village Square wall quilt

Karla Schulz, Jackson, Minn.

piecing

1 Make four diagonal four patch blocks, each 16½" x 16½".

2 Sew four blocks together so the diagonal four patches create a square on point.

borders, see page 16

1 Sew Border #1 pieces to the sides, and then sew the remaining Border #1 pieces to the top and bottom of the blocks.

2 Sew Border #2 pieces to the sides of the blocks.

3 Sew an accent square to each end of the remaining borders. Press toward to the squares. Sew to the top and bottom of the quilt.

Note: *The large spaces in this quilt offer room for fancy stitching or appliqué.*

finishing, see page 17

1 Sandwich, quilt, and then bind your quilt with 2¾" wide binding strips pieced to measure 175".

2 Sign and date your quilt.

size: 40" x 40"

materials

- Light background fabric for blocks and border #2, 1½ yard
- Accent or scraps for blocks and border #1, ½ yard
- Diagonal triangle borders, ½ yard
- Backing, 1½ yards
- Batting, 44" x 44"
- Binding, ½ yard

Block Box #6
Snowflake

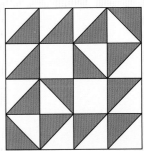

Please, review Half-Square Triangles, page 12. Directions are for one block. Make the number of blocks indicated for your size quilt.

- From light background fabric cut:
    - 7 squares, 3" x 3"
    - 2 squares, 2 1/2" x 2 1/2"
- From accent fabric cut:
    - 7 squares, 3" x 3"

1 Make 14 half-square triangles from 3" squares (2½" x 2½").

2 Sew two half squares and two squares together in pairs. Make two (2½" x 4½").

3 Sew four half squares together in pairs. Make two (2½" x 4½").

4 Sew pairs together to make two four patches (41/2" x 41/2").

5 Sew the remaining half squares together in pairs. Make four (2½" x 4½").

6 Sew pairs together. Make two (4½" x 4½").

7 Arrange the four patches in rows, and sew them together to complete the block (8½" x 8½").

8 Use the block to make the Snowflake Pillow, or make two blocks and put aside for the Prairie Sampler.

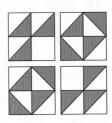

A Snowflake pillow makes a cheerful addition to any piece
of furniture.

Snowflake Pillow

Johanna Wilson, Walnut Grove, Minn.
Brenda Lee, Madison, S.D.

cutting

	Number of Strips	Size to cut strips WOF	Number of Pieces	Size of Pieces
Background—Light				
Blocks	2	3"	7	3" x 3"
			2	$3\frac{3}{4}$" x $3\frac{3}{4}$"
Border #2	1	$1\frac{3}{4}$"	2	$1\frac{3}{4}$" x 10"
			2	$1\frac{3}{4}$" x $12\frac{1}{2}$"
Blue Blocks	2	3"	7	3" x 3"
			2	$3\frac{3}{4}$" x $3\frac{3}{4}$"
Border # 3	2	$2\frac{3}{4}$"	4	$2\frac{3}{4}$" x $12\frac{1}{4}$"
Accent Border #1			2	$1\frac{1}{4}$" x $8\frac{1}{2}$"
			2	$1\frac{1}{4}$" x 10"
Backing	1	18"	2	18" x 21"
Binding				

size: 16" x 16"

materials

- Light background blocks and border fabric, 18" x 22"
- Accent border scraps
- Blue fabric for blocks and border, 18" x 22"
- Backing, $\frac{1}{2}$ yard
- Batting, 16" x 16"
- Binding, $\frac{1}{4}$ yard
- #7 embroidery needle
- Permanent marking pens (optional)

piecing

1 Make one blue Snowflake block.

2 From the two 3¾" squares, make four half-square triangles. Trim each to 2¾". Set aside.

3 Sew the 1¼" x 8½" accent borders (#1) to the sides of the block. Press toward the border.

4 Sew the 1¼" x 10" accent borders to the top and bottom of the block. Press toward the border.

5 Sew the 1¾" borders (#2) in the same manner.

6 Measure and cut two lengthwise and two crosswise borders (#3). Sew the lengthwise borders to the sides of the block. Sew a half square to each end of the crosswise borders. Sew to the top and bottom of the quilt.

7 Sandwich and quilt the pillow if desired.

pillow backs, see page 15

1 Fold the back pieces wrong sides together to measure 18" x 10½".

2 Overlap the folded ends to measure 18" x 18".

3 Center the pillow top right side up over the pillow backs. Baste the edges. Trim to 16½" x 16½".

finishing, see page 17

1 Bind your quilt with 2½" wide binding strips pieced to measure 75".

2 Sign and date your quilt.

Snowflake Quilts

The Snowflake quilt shown uses a different red or blue
fabric for each block until I ran out of half-square
triangles and used what was on hand—just like Grandma
would have done. That worked well too!

Snowflake Quilts

Johanna Wilson, Walnut Grove, Minn.
Quilted by Bonnie Erickson, Granite Falls, Minn.

size:

Wall Quilt:
44" x 56"

Twin Quilt:
64" x 84"

Queen Quilt:
94" x 94"

materials

	Wall Quilt	Twin Quilt	Queen Quilt
Finished Size	44" x 56"	64" x 84"	94" x 94"
Background—Light Blocks and Border	$2^3/_4$ yards	5 yards	$7^1/_2$ yards
Blue Blocks	$^5/_8$ yard	1 yard	$1^3/_4$ yards
Red Blocks	$^5/_8$ yard	1 yard	$1^3/_4$ yards
Backing	3 yards	$4^1/_2$ yards	$7^1/_2$ yards
Batting	48" x 60"	69" x 78"	88" x 98"
Binding	$^1/_2$ yard	$^3/_4$ yard	1 yard

cutting for the Snowflakes wall quilt

	Number of Strips	Size to cut strips WOF	Number of Pieces	Size of Pieces
Background—Blocks	9	3"	112	3" x 3"
Sashing	7	$2^1/_2$''	3	$2^1/_2$" x $28^1/_2$"
			8	$2^1/_2$" x $8^1/_2$"
			32	$2^1/_2$" x $2^1/_2$"
Borders, cut lengthwise	4	$8^1/_{12}$"		
Blue	4	3"	56	3" x 3"
Red	4	3"	56	3" x 3"
Binding	6	$2^1/_2$"		

cutting for the Snowflakes twin quilt

	Number of Strips	Size to cut strips WOF	Number of Pieces	Size of Pieces
Background				
Blocks	20	3"	273	3" x 3"
Sashing	11	$2^1/_2$''	28	$2^1/_2$" x $8^1/_2$"
			78	$2^1/_2$" x $2^1/_2$"
Blue	11	3"	154	3" x 3"
Red	9	3"	119	3" x 3"
Border	8	$8^1/_2$"		
Binding	8	$2^3/_4$"		

cutting for the Snowflakes queen quilt

	Number of Strips	Size to cut strips WOF	Number of Pieces	Size of Pieces
Background—Blocks, Sashing	34	3"	476	3" x 3"
	20	2½''	56	2½" x 8½"
			138	2½" x 2½"
Crosswise sashing	16	2½"		
Blue	174	3"	238	3" x 3"
Red	174	3"	238	3" x 3"
Borders	10	8½"		
Binding	10	2¾"		

Make the number of Snowflake blocks indicated for the desired size quilt.

Snowflake blocks	Wall Quilt	Twin Quilt	Queen Quilt
Blue	8	22	34
Red	8	17	34

piecing

Directions are for the wall quilt. Bed quilt changes are in parentheses (twin, queen).

1 Arrange 16 (39, 68) Snowflake blocks and 8 (28, 56) 2½" sashing strips in rows. Sew the rows together.

2 Sew 2½" sashing strips between the rows.

borders, see page 16

1 Measure and cut lengthwise and crosswise borders. Sew the lengthwise borders to the sides of the quilt.

2 Sew a Snowflake block to each end of the crosswise borders. Sew one border to the top and one to the bottom of the quilt.

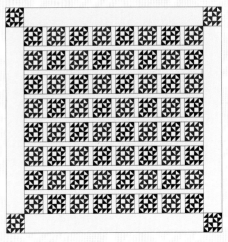

finishing, see page 17

1 Sandwich, quilt, and then bind your quilt with 2½" (2¾", 2¾") wide binding strips pieced to measure 75" (225", 400").

2 Sign and date your quilt.

Block Box #7
Stars and Stripes

piecing

Please, review Double Flip Corner, page 15. Directions are for two Stars and Stripes blocks. Make the number of blocks indicated for your size quilt.

1 Sew a 2½" accent square on the diagonal to opposite corners of the center square. Be sure the angle matches the illustration. Trim the inner triangle, press, flip, and press again. Make two. ***Note:*** *I like to cut the underside of the triangle, leaving the base piece (square, rectangle, etc.) in the original shape to act as a stabilizer for sewing on to the next piece. This is another way to help maintain accuracy when sewing smaller pieces together.*

2 Sew a 2" accent square on the diagonal to each 2½" x 4½" background rectangle.

3 Sew one background rectangle to each side of the 4" center square (8½" x 4½").

4 Sew a 2" accent square on the diagonal to each 2½" x 6½" background rectangle. Be sure the angle matches the illustration. Sew a 2" background square to the accent triangle. Make two (2½" x 8½").

cutting

- From medium background fabric cut:
    - 4 squares, 2½" x 2½"
    - 4 rectangles, 2½" x 4½"
    - 4 rectangles, 2½" x 6½"
    - 1 square, 9" x 9"
- From center fabric cut:
    - 2 squares, 4½" x 4½"
- From accent fabric cut:
    - 12 squares, 2½" x 2½"
- From contrasting fabric cut:
    - 1 square, 9" x 9"

5 Sew to the top and bottom of the center square. Make two (8½" x 8½").

6 Set the squares aside to use for the Patriotic Table Runner.

7 Make two half-square triangles from the 9" squares. Trim them to 8½".

8 Arrange and sew the Stars and Stripes blocks and half squares in rows.

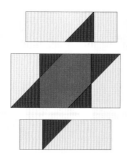

9 Sew the rows together (16½" x 16½").

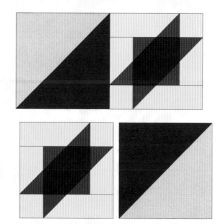

10 Set aside for the Prairie Sampler.

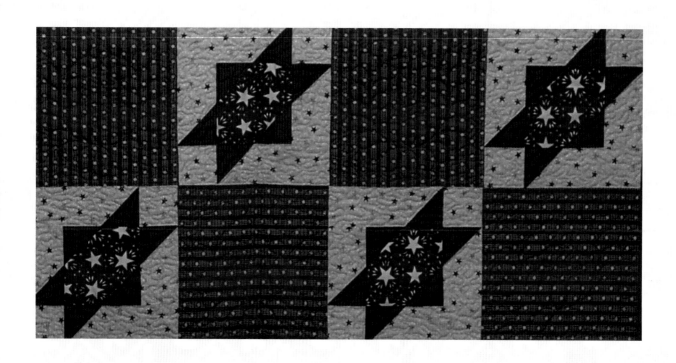

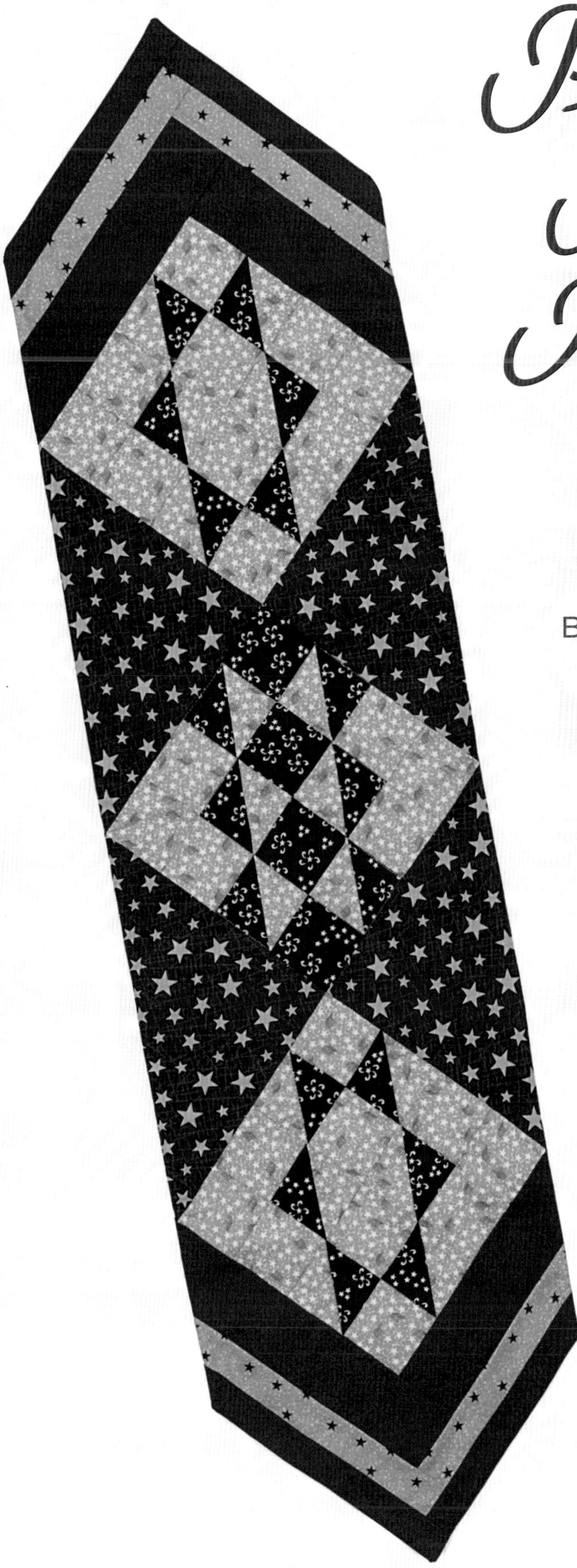

Patriotic Table Runner

Blocks on point sparkle
when bright setting
triangles and stripe
borders are added.

Patriotic Table Runner

Edie Pearson, Grand Marsh, Wis.
Quilted by Karla Schulz, Jackson, Minn.

size: 11¼" x 46"

materials

- Darks/navy, 18" x 22"
- Light fabrics for background, ⅓ yard
- Setting triangles, 18" x 22"
- Accent borders, 18" x 22"
- Backing, ½ yard
- Batting, 15" x 48"
- Binding, ⅓ yard (optional)

cutting

	Number of Strips	Size to cut strips WOF	Number of Pieces	Size of Pieces
Lights—				
Blocks		3"	2	3" x 3"
			2	2½ x 4½"
			2	2" x 2 "
Borders		1½"	2	1½" x 9"
			2	1½" x 11½"
Darks—Four Patch and stars		3	4	2½" x 2½"
			3	3" x 3"
Setting Triangles			1	11¾" cut diagonally twice
Accent Borders		2½"	2	2½" x 9"
			2	2½" x 11½"
		1½"	2	1½" x 9"
			2	1½" x 11½"
Binding optional*	4	2½"		

The table runner pictured does not have binding. It was finished by sewing the pieced top with batting to the backing, right sides together, leaving a 12" opening. Right sides were turned out and closed with a slip-stitch. Quilting was done after the runner was completed.

Make the number of blocks indicated for the Patriotic Table Runner.

	Star blocks	Double four patch
Blocks	2	1

piecing the Double Four Patch

1. Make six half-square triangles from dark and light 3" squares. Trim to measure 2½".

2. Sew a triangle square to a dark square. Make four (2½" x 4½").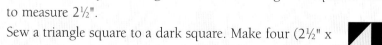

3 Sew two pairs together. Make two (4½" x 4 ½").

4 Sew a half square triangle and a light square together. Make two (2½" x 4½").

5 Sew a light rectangle to the top of each pair. Make two (4½" x 4½").

6 Arrange and sew the blocks to make a four patch. Make one (4½" x 4½").

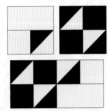

7 Arrange the two star blocks, the four patch, and the large triangles in rows, matching at the inside corner. The large triangles will extend beyond the outside edge. Sew each row together with the triangle on the bottom whenever possible to avoid stretching the bias edge.

8 Press carefully toward the large triangle. Triangles will be trimmed in step 13.

9 Sew the rows together, matching the centers. Press.

10 Sew the 2½" x 9" accent border pieces to opposite ends of the blocks. Press toward the border.

11 Sew the 2½" x 11½" accent border to adjacent sides of the same blocks.

12 Repeat with the background fabric and the accent borders, pressing toward the dark fabric after each addition.

13 Place a line of a long ruler through the center of the four patches so that the side extends ¼" beyond the intersections of the triangles along the outside edge of a runner. Use a rotary cutter to trim the excess.

finishing, see page 17

1 Sandwich, quilt, and then bind your quilt with 2½" wide binding strips pieced to measure 140".

2 Sign and date your quilt.

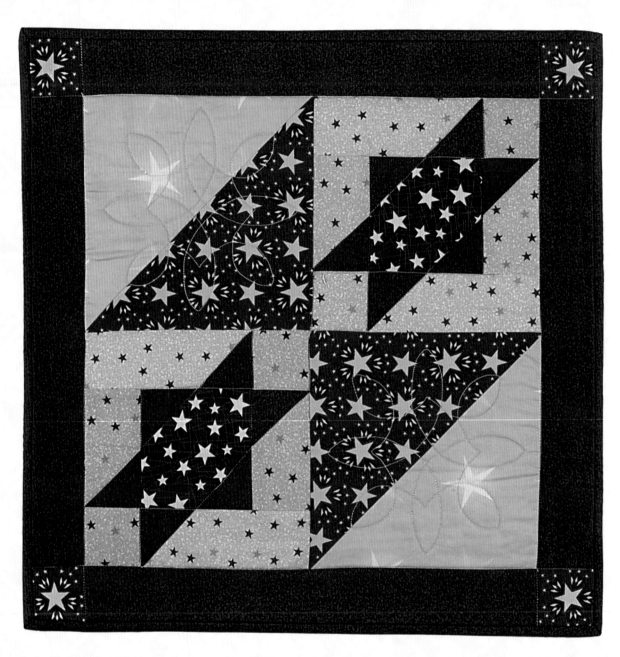

Make this quick quilt to celebrate a holiday or special event. The large triangles can be filled with fancy stitches or an appliqué star or two. Ours has star fabric fussy cut so the stars are in the center of the triangles.

Patriotic Wall Quilt

Johanna Wilson, Walnut Grove, Minn.
Quilted by Karla Schulz, Jackson, Minn.

blocks

size: 20" x 20"

Piece one Stars and Stripes block.

piecing

1 Cut four border strips 2½" x 16½".

2 Cut four corner squares 2½" x 2½".

3 Sew a border strip to opposite sides of the quilt. Press toward the border.

4 Sew a corner square to each end of the remaining strips. Press toward the border.

5 Sew one border to the top and one to the bottom of the quilt.

finishing, see page 17

Sandwich, quilt, and then bind your quilt with 2½" wide binding strips pieced to measure 100".

Note: *This block also makes a large decorative pillow. See Pillow Backs, page 15.*

The Stars and Stripes quilt is a favorite of mine because I love to use stripe fabric in my quilts. Changing the orientation of the stripes in the alternate blocks adds visual interest to the design. I also like the bold stripes framing the quilt. You might prefer to have the stripes run perpendicular to the blocks and have a very different look! For an example, see the stripe version of the Variable Star, page 110.

Stars and Stripes

Johanna Wilson, Walnut Grove, Minn.
Quilted by Bonnie Erickson, Granite Falls, Minn.

materials

	Lap Quilt	Twin Quilt	Queen Quilt
Finished Size	58" x 58"	75" x 90"	92" x 108"
Star Center	³⁄₈ yard	³⁄₄ yard	1 yard
Star Points	¹⁄₂ yard	1 yard	1¹⁄₂ yards
Background	³⁄₄ yard	2 yards	3 yards
Alternate Squares, Stripe	³⁄₄ yard	2 yards	3¹⁄₄ yards
Inner Border	¹⁄₄ yard	¹⁄₂ yard	³⁄₄ yard
Outer Border, cut lengthwise	1¹⁄₄ yards	2¹⁄₄ yards	2¹⁄₂ yards
Backing	3¹⁄₂ yards	5¹⁄₄ yards	7¹⁄₂ yards
Batting	64" x 64"	81" x 97"	98" x 114"
Binding	¹⁄₂ yard	³⁄₄ yard	1 yard

size:

Lap Quilt:
58" x 58"

Twin Quilt:
75" x 90"

Queen Quilt:
92" x 108"

cutting for the Stars and Strips lap quilt

	Number of Strips	Size to cut strips WOF	Number of Pieces	Size of Pieces
Star Center	2	4¹⁄₂"	17	4¹⁄₂" x 4¹⁄₂"
Star Points	7	2¹⁄₂"	102	2¹⁄₂" x 2¹⁄₂"
Background	14	2¹⁄₂"	34	2¹⁄₂ x 6¹⁄₂"
			34	2¹⁄₂" x 4¹⁄₂"
			34	2¹⁄₂" x 2¹⁄₂"
Alternate Blocks, Stripe	3	8¹⁄₂"	12	8¹⁄₂" x 8¹⁄₂"
Inner border	4	1¹⁄₂"		
Stripe border	Lengthwise 4	8¹⁄₂"		
Binding	6	2¹⁄₂"		

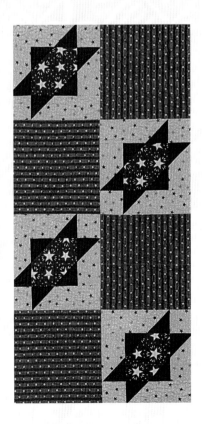

cutting for the Stars and Stripes twin quilt

	Number of Strips	Size to cut strips WOF	Number of Pieces	Size of Pieces
Star Center	5	4½"	36	4½" x 4½"
Star Points	14	2½"	216	2½" x 2½"
Background	26	2½"	72	2½ x 6½"
			72	2½" x 4½"
			72	2½" x 2½"
Alternate Blocks, Stripe	8	8½"	31	8½" x 8½"
Inner Border	7	2"		
Stripe Border	Lengthwise 4	8½"		
Binding	9	2¾"		

cutting for Stars and Strips queen quilt

	Number of Strips	Size to cut strips WOF	Number of Pieces	Size of Pieces
Star center	7	4½"	54	4½" x 4½"
Star points	21	2½"	324	2½" x 2½"
Background	38	2½"	108	2½" x 6½"
			108	2½" x 4½"
			108	2½" x 2½"
Alternate blocks, stripe	13	8½"	49	8½" x 8½"
Inner border	8	2½"		
Stripe border	Lengthwise 4	8½"		
Binding	11	2¾"		

piecing

Make the number of blocks indicated for the desired size quilt.

	Lap Quilt	Twin Quilt	Queen Quilt
Star blocks	17	36	54

quilt construction

Directions are for the lap quilt. Bed quilt changes are in parentheses (twin, queen).

1 Arrange 17 (36, 54) star blocks and 12 (31, 49) alternate squares in rows. Note the orientation of the pieced and stripe blocks as the stripes change direction in each row. Sew the blocks together in rows. Press each pieced block toward the alternate block.

2 Sew the rows together interlocking seams.

3 Measure and cut two lengthwise borders from accent fabric. Mark and match the centers of the quilt and the centers of the borders. Sew to the sides of the quilt. Press toward the borders.

4 Measure and cut two crosswise borders from accent fabric. Mark and match the centers of the quilt and the centers of the borders. Sew to the top and bottom of the quilt. Press toward the borders.

5 Measure and cut two lengthwise borders from outer border fabric. Measure and cut two crosswise borders from outer border fabric.

6 Mark and match the centers of the quilt and the centers of lengthwise borders. Sew borders to the sides of the quilt.

7 Sew a pieced star block to each end of the crosswise borders. Press toward the block.

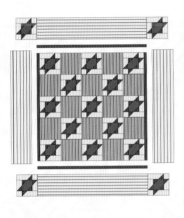
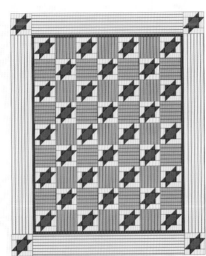

8 Mark, match, and sew the crosswise borders to the top and bottom of the quilt.

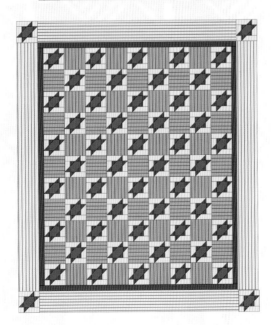

finishing, see page 17

1 Sandwich, quilt, and then bind your quilt with 2½" (2¾", 2¾") wide binding strips pieced to measure 250" (350", 415").

2 Sign and date your quilt.

Block Box #8
Flying Geese

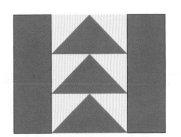

piecing

Please, review Double Flip Corners, page 15. Directions are for six blocks. Make the number of blocks indicated for your size quilt.

1 Sew a 2½" background square on the diagonal to each 2½" x 4½" rectangle. Trim the inner triangle, press, flip, and press. Repeat with a second square on the other end of each rectangle. Make three each color for each goose block (2½" x 4½").

2 Sew three geese of the same color together in formation (6½" x 8½").

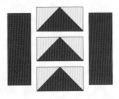

3 Sew a matching rectangle to both ends of each set of geese (6½" x 8½").

4 Sew six blocks together, and set them aside for the Prairie Sampler.

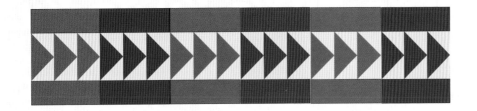

cutting

• From light background fabric cut:
  36 squares, 2½" x 2½"
• From each of six fabrics cut:
  3 rectangles, 2½ x 4½"
  2 rectangles, 2½" x 6½"

A large, colorful, scrappy pillow cover looks quite at home with or without the Migration quilt that follows!

cutting

	Number of Strips	Size to cut strips WOF	Number of Pieces	Size of Pieces
Background Scraps	6 each fabric	$2\frac{1}{2}$" x 16"	6	$2\frac{1}{2}$" x $2\frac{1}{2}$"
Geese Scraps	6 each fabric	$2\frac{1}{2}$" x 15"	18	$2\frac{1}{2}$" x $4\frac{1}{2}$"
		$2\frac{1}{2}$" x 14"	2	$2\frac{1}{2}$" x $6\frac{1}{2}$"
Border Scraps			6	3" x $8\frac{1}{2}$"
Border	3	5"	2	5" x $17\frac{1}{2}$"
			2	5" x $33\frac{1}{2}$"
Backing	1	36"	2	$20\frac{1}{2}$" x 36"
Binding	4	$2\frac{3}{4}$"		

Migration Pillow

Karla Schulz, Jackson, Minn.

piecing

1 Make six flying geese blocks.

2 Sew the blocks together in rows. Sew the rows together (24½" x 12½").

3 Arrange and sew three scraps (3" x 8½") together. Sew them to the top and bottom of the blocks.

borders, see page 16

1 Measure, cut, and sew the borders to the sides of the quilt.

2 Measure, cut, and sew the borders to the top and bottom of the quilt (34" x 25").

3 Sandwich and quilt if desired.

pillow backs, see page 15

1 Fold each pillow back wrong sides together to measure 20½" x 18". Stitch ⅜" from the folded edge.

2 Overlap the backs to measure 20½" x 33½".

3 Place the pillow top right side up on the pillow backs and baste together.

finishing, see page 17

1 Bind the quilt with 2¾" wide binding strips pieced to measure 135".

2 Sign and date your quilt.

size: 33" x 25"

materials

- Background scraps:
  for blocks, ¼ yard
  for borders, ½ yard
- Geese scraps:
  for blocks, ½ yard
- Backing, 1 yard
- Batting, 38" x 32"
- Binding, ½ yard

Karla loves to make quilts from scraps, and this is
a wonderful example of a great scrap quilt! She
then quilted it on her sewing machine. This is a
great way to try to use all your scraps!

Migration Quilts

Karla Schulz, Jackson, Minn.

materials

	Lap Quilt	Twin Quilt	Queen Quilt
Finished Size	60" x 76"	76" x 88"	92" x 100"
Background—Scraps			
Blocks	1 yard	$1\frac{1}{2}$ yard	2 yards
Borders	$2\frac{1}{4}$ yards	$2\frac{3}{4}$ yards	$4\frac{1}{4}$ yards
Geese—Scraps			
Blocks	$\frac{3}{4}$ yard	1 yard	$1\frac{1}{2}$ yards
Borders	$\frac{3}{4}$ yard	$\frac{7}{8}$ yard	1 yard
Backing	$3\frac{3}{4}$ yards	7 yards	$8\frac{1}{4}$ yards
Batting	66" x 80"	80" x 92"	94" x 104"
Binding	$\frac{3}{4}$ yard	$\frac{3}{4}$ yard	1 yard

size:

Lap Quilt:
60" x 76"

Twin Quilt:
76" x 88"

Queen Quilt:
92" x 100"

cutting for the Migration lap quilt

	Number of Strips	Size to cut strips WOF	Number of Pieces	Size of Pieces
Background Scraps				
Geese	12	$2\frac{1}{2}$"	180	$2\frac{1}{2}$" x $2\frac{1}{2}$"
			(6 per block)	
Borders	14	$6\frac{1}{2}$"	54	$6\frac{1}{2}$" x $8\frac{1}{2}$"
Corners			4	3" x 3"
Color Scraps				
Geese	30	$2\frac{1}{2}$" x 30"	3 per block	$2\frac{1}{2}$" x $4\frac{1}{2}$"
			2 per block	$2\frac{1}{2}$" x $6\frac{1}{2}$"
Borders	8	3"	24	3" x $6\frac{1}{2}$"
			14	3" x $8\frac{1}{2}$"
Binding	8	$2\frac{3}{4}$"		

cutting for the Migration twin quilt

	Number of Strips	Size to cut strips WOF	Number of Pieces	Size of Pieces
Background Scraps				
Geese	18	2½"	288	2½" x 2½"
			(6 per block)	
Borders	16	6½"	18	6½" x 8½"
Corners			4	3" x 3"
Color Scraps				
Geese	48	2½" x 30"	3	2½" x 4½"
			(each block)	
			78	2½" x 6½"
Borders	8	3"	28	3" x 6½"
	4	3"	18	3" x 8½"
Binding	9	2¾"		

cutting for the Migration queen quilt

	Number of Strips	Size to cut strips WOF	Number of Pieces	Size of Pieces
Background Scraps				
Blocks	27	2½"	420	2½" x 2½"
			(6 per block)	
Borders	27	6½"	102	6½" x 8½"
Corners			4	3" x 3"
Color Scraps	70	2½" x 30"	3	2½" x 4½"
			(each block)	
			2	2½" x 6½"
Borders	4	3"	22	3" x 6½"
	8	3"	32	3" x 8½"
			4	3" x 3"
Binding	11	2¾"		

piecing

Directions are for the lap quilt. Bed quilt sizes are in parentheses (twin, queen).

1 Make 30 (48, 70) Flying Geese blocks.

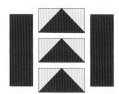 

2 Sew 10 (12, 14) blocks together in 3 (4, 5) columns. Press toward the top of the blocks in the same direction the geese are flying.

3 Sew 6½" x 8½" background border pieces together in 4 (5, 6) columns. Press toward the bottom of the columns. **Note:** *Pressing the seams in opposite directions will allow them to interlock as you sew the columns together.*

4 Sew the columns of Flying Geese and background scraps together, beginning and ending with background scraps.

5 Arrange and sew two rows of 7 (9, 11) background blocks (6½" x 8½") together. Sew one row to the top and one row to the bottom of the quilt.

6 Arrange and sew 12 (14, 16) colored scraps (3" x 6½") together. Press in the same direction as the geese are flying. Sew them to the sides of the quilt.

7 Arrange and sew 7 (9, 11) colored scraps (3" x 6½") together. Sew a 3" x 3" square to each end of each row. Sew the rows to the top and the bottom of the quilt.

piecing

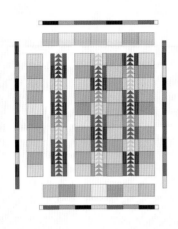

finishing, see page 17

1 Sandwich, quilt, and then bind the quilt with 2¾" wide binding strips pieced to measure 285" (340", 410").

2 Sign and date your quilt.

Block Box #9
Checkerboard Geese

piecing

Please, review Strip Piecing, page 12, and Double Flip Corners, page 15, to make the geese. Directions are for four blocks. Make the number of blocks indicated for your size quilt.

cutting

- From light background fabric cut:
    - 2 strips, 2½" x 22"
    - 8 rectangles, 2½" x 4½"
    - 16 squares, 2½" x 2½"
- From accent fabrics cut:
    - 2 strips, 2½" x 22"
    - 8 rectangles, 2½" x 4½"
    - 16 squares, 2½" x 2½"

checkerboard

1 Sew strips of two different fabrics together. Make two. Press toward the darker fabric. Sew two sections together, alternating dark and light fabrics. Press toward the darker fabric.

2 Cut at 2½" intervals. Make eight cuts.

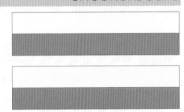

3 Sew a 2½" light square on the diagonal to each accent rectangle. Sew a second light square to the other end of the accent rectangle. Make eight geese (2½" x 4½").

4 Sew a 2½" accent square on the diagonal to each background rectangle. Sew a second accent square to the other end of the accent rectangle. Make eight geese (2½" x 4½").

5 Sew two geese together, alternating the dark and light fabrics. Make eight (4½" x 4½").

6 Sew two pairs of geese together, alternating the dark and light fabrics. Make four (4½" x 8½").

7 Sew a row of four squares from step 2 to each side of each geese block, alternating light and dark fabrics (8½" x 8½").

8 Sew the four blocks together in a row, alternating dark and light fabrics, for the Prairie Sampler.

In this variation of the Checkerboard Geese block, the pieced
geese have dark geese (red and navy) facing each other.
Background squares are used for all the geese.
The checkerboard strips alternate darks and lights
with the pieced geese.

cutting

	Number of Strips	Size to cut strips WOF	Number of Pieces	Size of Pieces
Background Blocks	2	$2\frac{1}{2}$"	32	$2\frac{1}{2}$" x $2\frac{1}{2}$"
Geese #1, Red	1	$2\frac{1}{2}$"	8	$2\frac{1}{2}$" x $4\frac{1}{2}$"
Geese #2, Navy	1	$2\frac{1}{2}$"	8	$2\frac{1}{2}$" x $4\frac{1}{2}$"
Checkerboard #1	1	$2\frac{1}{2}$"		
Checkerboard #2	1	$2\frac{1}{2}$"		
Sashing	4	$2\frac{1}{2}$"	2	$4\frac{1}{2}$" x $8\frac{1}{2}$"
			4	$2\frac{1}{2}$" x $8\frac{1}{2}$"
Borders			2	$2\frac{1}{2}$" x $12\frac{1}{2}$"
			2	$2\frac{1}{2}$" x $36\frac{1}{2}$
Binding	3	$2\frac{1}{2}$"		

Old Glory Table Runner

Kathy Goral, Stillman Valley, Ill.
Quilted by Brenda Lee, Madison, S.D.

piecing

size: 16" x 36"

1 Make four Checkerboard Geese blocks.

2 Sew 2½" x 8½" sashing strips to opposite ends of a checkerboard block. Make two (12½" x 8½").

3 Sew a 4½" x 8½" sashing to one end of each of the remaining blocks. Make two (12½" x 8½").

4 Arrange the blocks in a row, so that the squares create a checkerboard between the blocks. Sew the blocks together (12½" x 32½").

5 Sew 2½" x 8½" sashing to each end of the blocks (12½" x 36½").

6 Sew the 2½" x 36½" sashing strips to the sides of the blocks to complete the table runner (16½" x 36½").

materials

- Red fabric for Geese #1, ⅛ yard
- Navy fabric for Geese #2, ⅛ yard
- Scraps for background blocks, ¼ yard
- Checkerboard fabric #1, ⅛ yard
- Checkerboard fabric #2, ⅛ yard
- Sashing/borders, ⅓ yard
- Backing, 20" x 40"
- Batting, 20" x 40"
- Binding, ⅓ yard

finishing, see page 17

1 Sandwich, quilt, and then bind your quilt with 2½" wide binding strips pieced to measure 115".

2 Sign and date your quilt.

The pieced geese in this table runner have dark geese (red and navy) facing each other. Background squares are used for all the geese. The checkerboard strips alternate darks and lights with the pieced geese. This is a slight variation of the Block box.

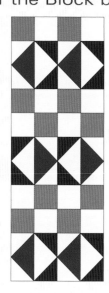

cutting

	Number of Strips	Size to cut strips WOF	Number of Pieces	Size of Pieces
Background				
Blocks			32	$2\frac{1}{2}$" x $2\frac{1}{2}$"
Sashing			2	$4\frac{1}{2}$" x $8\frac{1}{2}$"
			2	$2\frac{1}{2}$" x $16\frac{1}{2}$"
			2	$2\frac{1}{2}$" x $28\frac{1}{2}$"
Geese #1, Red			8	$2\frac{1}{2}$" x $4\frac{1}{2}$"
Geese #2, Navy			8	$2\frac{1}{2}$" x $4\frac{1}{2}$"
Checkerboard #1		$2\frac{1}{2}$"		
Checkerboard #2		$2\frac{1}{2}$"		
Borders	1	$6\frac{1}{2}$"	2	6" x $16\frac{1}{2}$"
Binding	3	$2\frac{1}{2}$"		

My Garden Spot Table Runner

Kathy Goral, Stillman Valley, Ill.
Quilted by Bonnie Erickson, Granite Falls, Minn.

piecing

1 Make four Checkerboard geese blocks.

2 Sew 4½" x 8½" sashing strips to opposite ends of a checkerboard block. Make two (8½" x 16½").

3 Sew two checkerboard blocks together, alternating the colors of the squares (8½" x 16½").

4 Arrange the blocks so that the colored squares create a checkerboard. Sew the blocks together (16½" x 24½").

5 Sew 2½" sashing strips to the ends of the blocks and then to the sides (20½" x 28½").

6 Sew 6½" border pieces to each end to complete the table runner (16½" x 40½").

size: 20" x 40"

materials

- Red fabric for Geese #1, ⅛ yard
- Navy fabric for Geese #2, ⅛ yard
- Scraps for background blocks, ¼ yard
- Checkerboard fabric #1, ⅛ yard
- Checkerboard fabric #2, ⅛ yard
- Sashing/borders, ⅓ yard
- End border, ¼ yard
- Backing, 24" x 44"
- Batting, 24" x 44"
- Binding, ⅓ yard

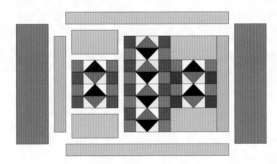

finishing, see page, 17

1 Sandwich, quilt, and then bind your quilt with 2½" wide binding strips pieced to measure 175".

2 Sign and date your quilt.

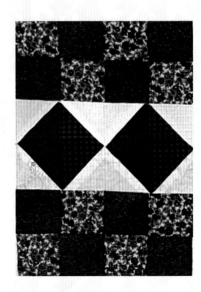

Block Box #10
Feathered Cross

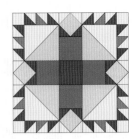

piecing

cutting

Please, review Double/Double Flip Corners, page 15. Directions are for one block. Make the number of blocks indicated for your size quilt.

1 Sew a 2½" light background square and a 2½" accent square on the diagonal to opposite corners of each 4½" medium background square. Trim, press, and flip corners. **Note:** *I like to leave the back piece and cut away the inside triangle. This adds stability to the shape of the piece.*

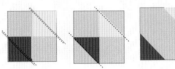

2 Sew a second pair of squares to the remaining corners. Trim, press, and flip as in Step 1.

3 Sew squares with the four flip corners to each 4½" dark square with the point toward the 4½" square. Make four (4½" x 8½").

4 Make half squares from 7" light background and medium background squares. Trim to 6½". Make four.

5 Make half squares from 3" light background squares and 3" accent squares. Trim to 2½". Make 24.

6 Sew three half squares together in a row. Sew the row with the small dark triangles to the light side of the 6½" half square. Make four (6½" x 8 ½").

7 Sew three half squares together. Note the angle of the triangles in the illustration. Add a background square to the dark triangle. Sew the row with the small dark triangles to the large light triangle. Make four (8½" x 8½").

8 Arrange the pieced blocks in rows, and sew them together (20½" x 20½").

9 Set the piece aside for the Prairie Sampler.

- From medium background fabric cut:
    - 2 squares, 7" x 7"
    - 4 squares, 4½" x 4½"
- From light background fabric cut:
    - 2 squares, 7" x 7"
    - 12 squares, 3" x 3"
    - 12 squares, 2½" x 2½"
- From dark fabric cut:
    - 4 squares, 4½" x 4½"
- From assorted accent fabrics cut:
    - 8 squares, 2½" x 2½"
    - 1 square, 4½" x 4½"
    - 12 squares, 3" x 3"

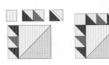
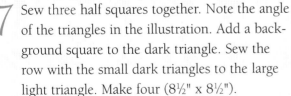
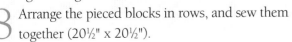
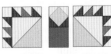

These quilts show that changing the color can be a dramatic statement.
They are also good examples of using stripe and plaid fabric.
Maybe they will encourage your creative juices to go into action!

cutting

	Number of Strips	Size to cut strips WOF	Number of Pieces	Size of Pieces
Background, Light				
Blocks	1	7"	2	7" x 7"
			12	3" x 3"
		2½"	8	2½" x 2½"
Sashing	3	2"	2	2" x 20½"
			2	2" x 24½"
Background, Medium				
Pieced Border	2	7"	10	7" x 7"
Blocks	1	4"	4	4½" x 4½"
Border #2	4	2"		
Dark fabric				
Pieced border	2	7"	10	7" x 7"
Blocks	1	4½"	4	4½" x 4½"
Border #3	4	6"		
Accent Fabric, scraps				
Blocks	1	3"	12	3" x 3"
		2½"	8	2½" x 2½"
			1	4½" x 4½"
Border #1	4	2½"		
Binding	6	2½"		

Feathered Cross Wall Quilt

Karla Schulz, Jackson, Minn.
Quilted by Bonnie Erickson, Granite Falls, Minn.

piecing

Please, review Half-Square Triangles, page 12, and Double Flip Corners, page 15.

1 Make one Feathered Cross block.

2 Sew the 20½" sashing to the sides of the Feathered Cross block. Sew the 24½" borders to the top and the bottom of the block. Press toward the sashing.

3 Make 20 half-square triangles from the 7" dark and medium background squares. Trim to measure 6½". Arrange four blocks in a row, alternating colors. Make two (6½" x 24½"). Sew to the sides of the quilt with medium triangles toward the sashing.

4 Arrange six blocks in a row, alternating colors. Make two (6½" x 36½"). Sew them to the top and bottom of the quilt with medium triangles toward the sashing.

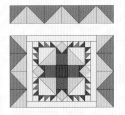

size: 52" x 52"

materials

- Light background fabric, ¾ yard
- Medium background fabric, 1 yard
- Dark fabric, 1¼ yard
- Assorted accent fabrics, ½ yard
- Backing, 3 yards
- Batting, 56" x 56"
- Binding, ½ yard

borders, see page 16

1 Measure, cut, and sew Border #1 to the sides of the quilt. Repeat with the top and bottom borders.

2 Repeat with Border # 2 and Border #3.

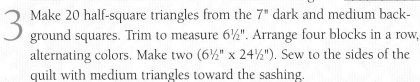

finishing, see page 17

1 Sandwich, quilt, and then bind your quilt with 2½" wide binding strips pieced to measure 220".

2 Sign and date your quilt.

Feathered Cross Queen Quilt

This is a stunning design, suitable for a large bed, that can be enlarged even more with the addition of a second plain border around the second pieced border. If you decide to make this quilt, please send us a picture.

size: 96" x 96"

materials

- Light background fabric, 1¾ yards
- Medium background fabric, 3 yards
- Dark fabric, 2¾ yards
- Accent fabric, 1½ yards
- Medium fabric for un-pieced border, 1¾ yards
- Backing, 7 yards
- Batting, 100" x 100"
- Binding, 1 yard

cutting

	Number of Strips	Size to cut strips WOF	Number of Pieces	Size of Pieces
Background, Light				
Blocks	2	7"	8	7" x 7"
	4	3" x 3"	48	3" x 3"
Sashing #1	12	2½"	8	2½ x 20½"
			8	2½" x 24½"
Blocks			24	2½" 2½"
Background, Medium				
Blocks	13	7"	78	7" x 7"
Pieced border	2	4½"	16	4½" x 4½"
Background, Dark				
Blocks	12	7"	70	7" x 7"
Pieced Border	2	4½"	16	4½" x 4½"
Accent fabric				
Feather points	3	3"	48	3" x 3"
	2	2½"	48	2½" x 2½"
Cross Centers	1	4½"	4	4½" x 4½"
Sashing #2	6	2½"	2	2½" x 36½"
			1	2½" x 74½"
Border Squares	1	7"	4	7" x 7"
Outer Border	8	7"		
Binding	10	2¾"		

1 Make four Feathered Cross blocks (20½" x 20½").

2 Sew a 2½" x 20½" sashing to each side of each block. Press toward the sashing.

piecing

3 Sew a 2½" x 24½" sashing to the top and bottom of each block. Press toward the sashing (24½" x 24½").

4 Make 80 half-square triangles from the 7" dark and medium background squares. Trim to measure 6½". Arrange four blocks in a row, creating a zigzag pattern. Make eight (6½" x 24½"). Sew them to the sides of each block with medium triangles toward the sashing.

5 Arrange six blocks in a row, creating a zigzag pattern. Make eight (6½" x 36½"). Sew them to the top and bottom of each block with medium triangles toward the sashing. Make four (36½" x 36½").

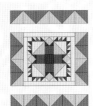

6 Sew 2½" x 36½" sashing strips between pairs of blocks. Press toward the sashing. Make two.

7 Sew two 2½" WOF sashing strips together. Measure and cut to 2½" x 74½".

8 Sew a 2½" x 74½" sashing strip between the rows of blocks. Press toward the sashing.

borders

The border pieces are cut an inch wider than is mathematically correct to allow for individual sewing. The quilt top, including the next border, will be trimmed to 84½" x 84½". It is necessary for the quilt to be the exact measurement in order to have the outer pieced border fit properly.

1 Measure and cut two lengthwise and two crosswise borders. Sew the lengthwise borders to the sides of the block.

2 Sew a 7" square to each end of the crosswise borders. Sew the borders to the top and bottom of the quilt. Press carefully toward the border. Trim the quilt to measure 84½" x 84½".

3 Make 60 half-square triangles from the 7" dark and medium background squares. Trim to measure 6½". Arrange 14 blocks in a row, creating a zigzag pattern. Make four (6½" x 84½"). Sew two sets to the sides of the quilt with the dark triangles toward the quilt.

4 Sew one block to each end of the two remaining borders. Sew the borders to the top and bottom of the quilt with the dark triangles toward the quilt (96½" x 96½").

finishing, see page 17

1 Sandwich, quilt, and then bind your quilt with 2½" wide binding strips pieced to measure 410".

2 Sign and date your quilt.

Block Box #11
Variable Star

piecing

Please, review Quarter Square Triangles, page 13, Half-square triangles, page 12, and Setting Triangles, page 14. Directions are for one block. Make the number of blocks indicated for your size quilt.

1 Make half-square triangles from the 5" squares. Trim to 4½". Make four.

2 Make quarter square triangles from the 6" squares. Make eight to measure 4½".

quilt construction

1 Sew a 4½" light square to each quarter-square triangle block. Make four (4½" x 8½").

2 Sew a 4½" half-square triangle to a quarter-square triangle block. Make four (4½" x 8½").

3 Sew pairs together to make a four patch. Make four (8½" X 8½").

4 Sew the background sashing strips between the four patches in the top and bottom rows. Press toward the sashing.

5 Sew a 2½" square between the remaining sashing strips. Press toward the strip.

6 Sew the rows together (18½" x 18½").

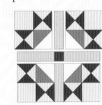

setting triangles

1 Cut the 13¾" squares in half diagonally.

2 Mark and match the center of the triangle to the center of opposite sides of the block. Press toward the triangle. Sew the remaining triangles in same manner. Trim the block to 26".

3 Set the block aside for the Prairie Sampler.

cutting

- From light background fabric cut:
    - 2 squares, 5" x 5"
    - 4 squares, 4½" x 4½"
    - 4 squares, 6" x 6"
- From medium background fabric:
    - 4 sashing rectangles, 2½" x 8½"
- From dark background fabric cut:
    - 2 squares, 5" x 5"
    - 2 squares, 13¾" x 13¾"
- From Accent fabric for center and star cut:
    - 1 square, 2½" x 2½"
    - 4 squares, 6" x 6"

The rich vibrant colors of fall sparkle in this seasonal quilt.
Large triangles showcase Bonnie's fancy stitching.

cutting

	Number of Strips	Size to cut strips WOF	Number of Pieces	Size of Pieces
Background, Light				
Setting Triangles	1	13¾"	2	13¾" x 13¾"
Blocks			2	5" x 5"
Background, Medium				
Blocks	1	5"	4	5" x 5"
			4	4½" x 4½"
Background, Dark				
Blocks	1	6"	4	6" x 6"
	1	2½"	4	2½" x 8½"
Star Points	1	6"	4	6" x 6"
Border #1	4	1½"	1	2½" x 2½"
Border #2	4 lengthwise	6½"		
Binding	6	2½"		

Autumn Beauty Quilt

Karla Schulz, Jackson, Minn.
Quilted by Bonnie Erickson, Granite Falls, Minn.

piecing

size: 40" x 40"

Piece one block according to the block box.

border, page 16

1 Measure, cut, and sew the Border #1 pieces to the sides of the quilt. Press toward the borders. Repeat with the top and bottom borders.

2 Measure and cut four Border #2 pieces. Sew one to each long side of the quilt. Press toward the borders. Sew the corner squares to the ends of the remaining borders. Press toward the square. Sew the borders to the top and bottom of the quilt.

materials

- Light background fabric, $\frac{1}{2}$ yard
- Medium background fabric, $\frac{1}{4}$ yard
- Dark background fabric, $\frac{1}{4}$ yard
- Fabric for star points, $\frac{1}{4}$ yard
- Border #1, $\frac{1}{4}$ yard
- Border #2, $1\frac{1}{4}$ yards
- Batting, 44" x 44"
- Backing, $1\frac{1}{4}$ yards
- Binding, $\frac{1}{2}$ yard

finishing, see page, 17

1 Sandwich, quilt, and then bind you quilt with 2½" wide binding strips pieced to measure 175".

2 Sign and date your quilt.

The colors in this quilt remind me of a summer salad made of two of my favorite fruits—blueberries and raspberries—and two favorite blocks—pinwheels and quarter square triangles. This quilted combination of fruit will last longer than a bowl of fruit!

cutting

	Number of Strips	Size to cut strips WOF	Number of Pieces	Size of Pieces
Background, Light	4	3"	48	3" x 3"
Background, Medium				
Quarter Squares	8	6"	50	6" x 6"
Border #1	4	1½"		
Raspberry Fabric				
Blocks, Pinwheels,	4	3"	48	3" x 3"
Border #2	4	2½"		
Blueberry Fabric				
Blocks				
Quarter Squares	6	6"	50	6" x 6"
Border #3	4	3½"		

Summer Delight

Karla Schulz, Jackson, Minn.

piecing

size: 40" x 40"

Please, review Half-Square Triangles, page 12, and Quarter-Square Triangles, page 13.

1 Make half-square triangles from the 3" Raspberry squares. Trim to measure 2½". Make 48.

2 Sew two triangles together to make Raspberry Pinwheels. Make 24 (4½" x 4½").

3 Make Blueberry quarter-square triangles from the 6" squares. Trim to measure 4½". Make 25.

4 Arrange Raspberry pinwheels and Blueberry quarter squares in rows. Note the orientation of the quarter squares.

5 Sew the rows together (28½" x 28½").

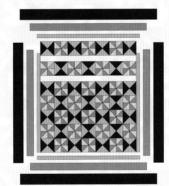

materials

- Light background fabric, ½ yard
- Medium fabric, 1½ yards
- Raspberry fabric, ¾ yard
- Blueberry fabric, 1½ yards

borders, see page 16

1 Measure, cut, and sew 1½" Border #1 strips to the sides of the quilt. Press toward the border.

2 Measure, cut, and sew 1½" Border #1 strips to the top and bottom of the quilt. Press toward the border.

3 Repeat with Border #2 and Border #3 (36½" x 36½").

finishing, see page 17

1 Sandwich, quilt, and then bind your quilt with 2½" wide binding strips pieced to measure 130".

2 Sign and date your quilt.

Prairie Sampler Quilts

Color Controlled Sampler

THE PLUM CREEK PRAIRIE SAMPLER includes two color variations. The original sample was made from fabric designed by Plum Creek Patchwork. This fabric is no longer available. However, the method of choosing fabrics for the quilt is one for you to consider as you decide your color scheme. This quilt is based on one focus fabric— floral, plaid, or medium to large-scale print—used as the outside border and in several of the blocks. Additional fabrics are chosen that blend with, not necessary match, the focus fabric. Be sure to vary the scale of your fabric choices to add interest. I used three background fabrics A-light, B-medium, and C-dark. These are letters indicated in the cutting directions as Background A, B, and C. These terms are relative, and you may choose three with much more or much less contrast than shown here.

materials

- At least a dozen quilter's quarters (18" x 22") of several colors in various shades to blend with your focus fabric. If you prefer a less scrappy look, six half yards will work just fine.
- Background fabrics (3 shades of your background choice with as much contrast as you wish)

  ¾ yard of light background (A)

  1½ yards of medium background (B)

  2½ yards of dark background (C, includes Border #2)
- Border fabrics

  3 yards of focus fabric for Border #3

  ⅝ yard of accent/contrast for Border #1

  1 yard for binding

Totally Scrappy Prairie Sampler

THE SECOND VERSION OF THE Prairie Sampler is a two-color quilt. The quilt is based on many shades of red, ranging from near pink to dark burgundy. The lights are many shades, ranging from off white to dark tan. This method works well for any color combination you choose. The shades do not have to match because they blend together well. The prints include small, medium, and large prints, stripes, geometrics, and a large check border. The border for this quilt was chosen after the top was pieced. The color was right and it added contrast to the blocks. The binding was a very small print that "reads" as a solid and frames the border well.

materials

- At least two dozen quilter's quarters (18" x 22") or as many scraps as you wish. Use more fabrics to achieve a scrappier look. Search your fabric collection, and stretch the color you have chosen by including many that do not necessarily match but when combined will blend. Some "uglies" may find a home in your quilt. Small pieces will add interest. Try one or two!
- Background fabric scraps to total:

  ¾ yard of light background (A)

  1½ yards of medium background (B)

  2½ yards of dark background (C, includes Border #1)
- Border fabrics

  3 yards of focus fabric for Border #3

  ⅝ yard of accent/contrast for Border #1

  1 yard for binding

quilt construction

Make the number of blocks indicated in each block box #1–11. You will need to cut sashing strips as you put the blocks together. They will fit together as a puzzle. If you find your blocks are not quite the correct size, you may adjust the size of the sashing strips accordingly. This is a way to be sure the pieces will fit together properly as you set the blocks together.

Block Box #1 *Windmill*, page 20

• From background C cut:
  1 sashing, 2" x 6½"
  1 sashing, 2" x 26"

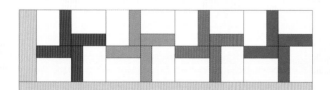

1 Sew the 2" x 6½" piece to the left end of the row of windmill blocks.

2 Sew the 2" x 26" piece to the bottom of the row of windmill blocks.

3 Set aside.

Block Box #2 *Tree*, page 34

No additional sashing needed.

Set aside.

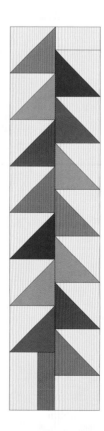

Block Box #3 *Four Patch/Broken Dishes*, page 40

• From background C cut:
  2 sashing, 1¾" x 20½"

1 Sew a sashing to the top and the bottom of the strip of blocks.

2 Set aside.

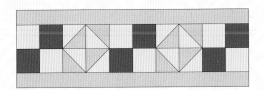

Block Box #4 *Pinwheel*, page 52

• For the Color Controlled Sampler, cut from Background C:
  1 rectangle, 4½" x 16½"

This block is shown differently in the two quilts. Look at each and decide whether you want the pinwheels in one row, as shown in the Color Controlled Sampler, or divided into two sections, as shown in the Scrappy Sampler.

Sew the rectangle to the top of the Pinwheel row in the Color Controlled version.

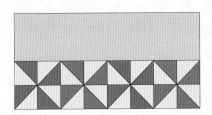

• For the Scrappy Sampler, cut from Background C:
  2 rectangles, 4½" x 8½"

Sew one rectangle to each pair of Pinwheels. Arrange the blocks together so the rectangle is at the top of one pair of Pinwheels and at the bottom of the other pair.

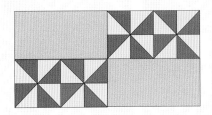

Block Box #5 *Diagonal Four Patch*, page 61

- For even sashings, as in photos on pages 114 and 116, from background C cut:
  2 sashing, 2½" x 16½"

OR

- For uneven sashings, as in illustrations on pages 120, 123, 125, and 126, from background C cut:
  1 sashing, 1¾" x 16½"
  1 sashing, 3¼" x 16½"

Compare the differences between the two options for sashing, and choose the one you like best for your quilt.

1 Sew sashing to each side of the block.

2 Sew the Diagonal Four Patch #4 to the top of the Broken Dishes/Four Patch #3

Block Box #6 *Snowflake*, page 68

• From background A cut:
  2 sashing, 2½" x 8½"

1 Sew sashing to the right side of each block.
   Sew the sections together.

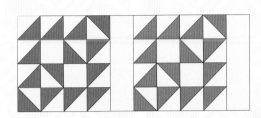

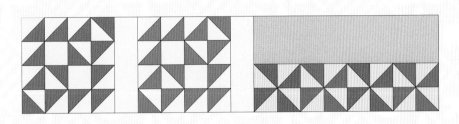

2 Sew the Snowflake
   blocks to the left
   side of the
   Pinwheel blocks
   (8½" x 36½").

Block Box #7 *Stars and Stripes*, page 76

• From background C cut:
  1 sashing, 2" x 16 ½"

1 Sew sashing to the left side of the block
   (18" x 16½").

2 Set aside.

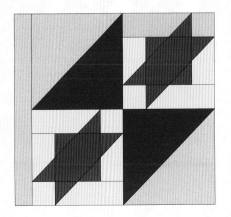

Block Box #8 *Flying Geese*, page 89

• From background C cut:
  1 sashing, 2½" x 54"

1 Sew the row of geese to the top of the Snowflake/Pinwheel section (16½" x 36½").

2 Sew the Stars and Stripes block to the right side (16½" x 54").

3 Sew a 2½" x 54" sashing from background C to the bottom of the row of blocks (18½" x 54"). This completes the top section of the Prairie Sampler quilt.

Block Box #9 Checkerboard Geese, page 96

• From background C cut:
  1 sashing, 2" x 8½"
  1 sashing, 2" x 34"

1 Sew the 8½" sashing to the left end of the blocks.

2 Sew the 34" sashing to the top of the blocks.

3 Set aside.

Block Box #10 *Feathered Cross*, page 102

No additional sashing needed.

Set aside.

Sew the Feathered Cross block to the bottom of the Diagonal Four Patch and Broken Dishes blocks (20½" x 43"). This completes another section of the Prairie Sampler quilt.

Block Box #11 *Variable Star*

1 Sew the Windmill blocks to the top of the Variable Star block.

2 Sew the Tree block to the left of the Windmill/Variable Star blocks.

3 Sew the Checkerboard Geese to the bottom of the blocks (34" x 43").

4 This completes the last section of the quilt.

complete the quilt top

Complete the Quilt top by sewing the three sections together.

- From border #1 fabric cut:
  7 crosswise strips 2½" wide
- From border #2 fabric cut:
  8 crosswise strips 3½" wide
- From border #3 fabric cut:
  4 strips lengthwise up to 10½" wide x
  approximately 95" long

borders, page 16

1 Measure, cut, and sew Border #1 to the left and right sides. Repeat with borders for the top and bottom.

2 Sew Border #2 and #3 together side by side.

Measure, cut, and sew the borders to the left and right sides. Repeat with the top and bottom.

finishing, see page 17

1 Sandwich, quilt, and then bind your quilt with 2¾" wide binding strips pieced to measure 400".

2 Sign and date your quilt.

Congratulations! You have finished your Prairie Sampler Quilt. Enjoy!

Johanna Wilson (Jo) grew up in New England where she became a teacher and high school librarian. In December of 1979, she and her husband, Ormon, moved to the plains of southwestern Minnesota to begin a new life on their prairie farm. Among the treasures they brought from Connecticut was a quilt top given to Johanna by a friend whose grandmother, Henrietta St. Dennis Buck, had pieced it back in the 1930s. The top remained packed for several years while Jo and Ormon remodeled the old farmhouse, began to work the land, and learned to garden and "put up" for winter.

The approach of a winter storm in 1984 prompted Jo's decision to try to quilt Henrietta's pieced top. With little knowledge of the quilting process, but with much determination, Jo attached the quilt to a frame Ormon had created with C-clamps and old pine boards. Throughout the long winter, large and uneven stitches were lovingly sewn to hold the layers together. As the quilting progressed, Johanna began to feel a kinship with Henrietta and questions arose about the block: its origins, its name, and the process by which it was made with its vivid colors and those red squares with large white polka dots in each corner!

After learning that it was called a "Fox and Geese" block, Jo began to explore more quilt blocks, their various names and the entire history and process of quilting. A desire to pursue this artform led her to begin designing quilts and publishing books with the establishment of PLUM CREEK PATCHWORK in 1992. In the intervening years, Jo's designs accompanied by Ormon's illustrations have been featured in eight self-published books and numerous patterns. Johanna has appeared on national television, been featured in many national quilt magazines, and developed her reputation as a well-known teacher of quilting. Her classes, trunk shows, and annual Plum Creek Quilt Retreats are known for her personal touch and her ability to instill confidence in novice quilters and to enhance the skills of experienced quilters. Her goal is for everyone to experience the satisfaction of making a quilt, and she strives to make the process do-able for all with clear directions and numerous illustrations. For those unable to commit to making a quilt, Jo encourages you to appreciate our quilting history and the art of quilting.

This year, Marcia Miles, Henrietta's granddaughter, attended the Plum Creek Quilt Retreat and made her first quilt. And so, the quilting circle widens and embraces another. What a thrill for all who attended.

For more information about Plum Creek Quilt Retreats visit our Web site at www.plumcreekpatchwork.com, or write

Plum Creek Patchwork
Johanna Wilson
14160 CO Hwy. 5
Walnut Grove, MN 56180

about the author

More Inspiring Ideas and New Techniques for Quilters

Raw Edge Appliqué
by Jodie Davis

You'll find 10 fun and fast quilt projects that eliminate hours of pinning and matching by using a straight machine stitch. The raw edges are left exposed to become slightly frayed as the quilt is loved, washed, and dried-and then loved some more. Features easy-to-follow instructions, detailed illustrations, and gorgeous photos of the finished quilts.

Softcover • 8¼x10⅞ • 96 pages
20 color photos
Item# FEQ • $19.95

The Essential Guide to Practically Perfect Patchwork
by Michele Morrow Harer

Beginning with the basics of quilting and then expanding to more advanced concepts, each of the 10 lessons builds on the previous one and allows even the most novice quilter to create fabulous quilts. Both machine and hand quilting are covered in this generously illustrated, easy-to-follow guide.

Softcover • 8¼x10⅞ • 160 pages
300+ color photos and illus.
Item# PPPWK • $21.95

A Forest of Quilts
by Terrie Kralik

Incorporate natural-looking trees and animals into gorgeous outdoorsy quilts and décor. Includes full-size patterns for moose, deer, bears, trees, flowers, and many others. Ten main projects highlight a different motif in each. Then mix and match the designs to create pillows, a tablecloth and embellish clothing.

Softcover • 8¼x10⅞ • 128 pages
50 color photos • 75+ illustrations
Item# FOQ • $21.99

Ragged-Edge Flowers
Fast-Folded Ways to Make Textured Quilts
by Laura Farson

You'll find more than 12 unique patterns for quilted wall hangings, pillow covers, and quilts. Instructions are easy-to-follow and the minimal sewing and "quilt-as-you-go" technique makes these 18 projects attainable for any skill level.

Softcover • 8¼x10⅞ • 96 pages
150+ color photos
Item# REF • $19.95

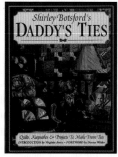

Daddy's Ties
by Shirley Botsford

Shirley Botsford unknots some creative ideas for Dad's old, unused ties. Learn to make great keepsakes and one-of-a-kind gifts. Complete patterns, step-by-step instructions, and full-color illustrations show you how to make quilts, picture frames, and dozens of other beautiful treasures.

Softcover • 8¼x10⅞ • 96 pages
color throughout
Item# DADTI • $16.95

Granny Quilts
Vintage Quilts of the '30s Made New for Today
by Darlene Zimmerman

Explore the history and style of the '30s quilts, while learning to replicate them with reproduction fabrics and 19 beautiful projects. A variety of appliquéd and pieced quilts are featured with updated rotary cutting directions written for quilters of all skill levels.

Softcover • 88¼x10⅞ • 128 pages
150+ color photos & illus.
Item# GRANQ • $21.95

Sizzling Quilts from a Simple Block
Hot, New Ideas for Woodpile Quilts
by Anita Hallock

Woodpile quilts are entirely strip-pieced-strips are pieced together, sectioned off, cut, and sewn again. Now you have an all-in-one resource for learning about this extremely fast and easy method of construction, once a substitute for the Log Cabin quilt style. Includes dozens of Design-Your-Own pages to create 25 masterpieces.

Softcover • 8½x11 • 160 pages
600 illus. • 48-page color section
Item# WOODQ • $21.95

The Quilter's Block Bible
by Celia Eddy

Create more than 150 individual quilt blocks and receive expert tips and techniques for creating your own quilt blocks in this spiral-bound guide. Learn how quilt blocks are categorized and follow selected examples from different categories to draft, design, and create custom patchwork. You'll receive great ideas, hints, and tips on layout, colors, and fabrics. Each block entry includes a photograph of the finished block, diagrams, and instructions for clear guidance.

Hardcover W/Concealed Spiral • 5¾x7¾ • 256 pages
150 color photos
Item# QBB • $29.99